Google Cloud Platform Cookbook

Implement, deploy, maintain, and migrate applications on Google Cloud Platform

Legorie Rajan PS

BIRMINGHAM - MUMBAI

Google Cloud Platform Cookbook

Copyright © 2018 Packt Publishing

Commissioning Editor: Vijin Boricha
Acquisition Editor: Heramb Bhavsar
Content Development Editor: Nithin Varghese
Technical Editor: Khushbu Sutar
Copy Editor: Safis Editing
Project Coordinator: Virginia Dias
Proofreader: Safis Editing
Indexer: Rekha Nair
Graphics: Tom Scaria
Production Coordinator: Shantanu Zagade

First published: April 2018

Production reference: 1120418

Published by Packt Publishing Ltd.
Livery Place
35 Livery Street
Birmingham
B3 2PB, UK.

ISBN 978-1-78829-199-6

www.packtpub.com

Dedicated to my Uncle and Godfather, Chinnappan S, who has shown me what work is—Karma Yogam.

– Legorie Rajan PS

`mapt.io`

Mapt is an online digital library that gives you full access to over 5,000 books and videos, as well as industry leading tools to help you plan your personal development and advance your career. For more information, please visit our website.

Why subscribe?

- Spend less time learning and more time coding with practical eBooks and Videos from over 4,000 industry professionals

- Improve your learning with Skill Plans built especially for you

- Get a free eBook or video every month

- Mapt is fully searchable

- Copy and paste, print, and bookmark content

PacktPub.com

Did you know that Packt offers eBook versions of every book published, with PDF and ePub files available? You can upgrade to the eBook version at `www.PacktPub.com` and as a print book customer, you are entitled to a discount on the eBook copy. Get in touch with us at `service@packtpub.com` for more details.

At `www.PacktPub.com`, you can also read a collection of free technical articles, sign up for a range of free newsletters, and receive exclusive discounts and offers on Packt books and eBooks.

Contributors

About the author

Legorie Rajan PS has 12 years of experience working in software development, business analysis, and project management. He is currently working as a cloud consultant on cloud migrations on AWS, Azure, and GCP. He has a rich multicultural experience working in India, the United States, and France. His other achievements are consulting for application migration to the Cloud, Certified AWS Solutions Architect, RHCE, and CEH. He has a good understanding of full-stack development, and has also been a technical reviewer for Packt.

I would like to thank my wife, Anitha Sophie, for being my rock. Also, special thanks to the reviewers and the team at Packt who have been the backbone in the formation of this book.

About the reviewers

Ted Hunter is a software engineering consultant and author of Google Cloud Platform for Developers. He works with fortune 500 companies to design cloud-native solutions and drive public cloud adoption, primarily within the Google ecosystem. He has a background in full stack development, DevOps transformation, and designing enterprise data solutions. He is currently a solutions architect at Slalom Consulting, serving clients in the Southeastern United States.

Chirag Nayyar is helping organizations to migrate their workload from on-premises to public cloud. He has experience ranging from web app migration, SAP workload on cloud, to EDW.

He is currently working with Cloud Kinetics Technology Solutions Pvt. Ltd. holding a wide range of certification from all major public cloud platforms. He is also running meetups and is a regular speaker on various cloud events.

Packt is searching for authors like you

If you're interested in becoming an author for Packt, please visit `authors.packtpub.com` and apply today. We have worked with thousands of developers and tech professionals, just like you, to help them share their insight with the global tech community. You can make a general application, apply for a specific hot topic that we are recruiting an author for, or submit your own idea.

Table of Contents

Preface

Google Cloud Platform (GCP) is a strong contender to the incumbents Amazon Web Services and Azure as the most prominent cloud service provider in the startup and enterprise world. When you think big, when you think about global scale and when you think about state-of-the art technology, the GCP will not let you down. The software and hardware, and the services built on them, come from Google's homegrown research. Both start-ups and enterprises now benefit from the wide array of services provided by GCP.

With GCP, it is easy to perform your business as usual using IaaS, PaaS, and container services backed with strongly supported networking, database offerings, and storage. GCP provides some unique services that are not available with any other provider, especially in managing huge volumes of data, machine learning, and AI.

The book covers a broad range of recipes to give you a taste of the GCP. If you are an architect, you'll find some interesting features of GCP that you can build upon. If you are a developer, you'll get your hands dirty on most of the important services and how to manage them programmatically.

Who this book is for

This book aims at IT professionals, engineers, and developers who are looking at implementing Google Cloud in their organizations. Administrators and architects planning to make their organization more efficient using Google Cloud will also find this book useful.

What this book covers

Chapter 1, *Compute*, contains recipes on the compute services of the GCP, namely Google Compute Engine, Google App Engine, Kubernetes Engine, and Google Cloud Functions.

Chapter 2, *Storage and Databases*, provides some recipes on Google Cloud Storage and some of the database options available (Cloud Spanner, Cloud BigQuery, Cloud Bigtable, and Cloud Datastore).

Chapter 3, *Networking*, provides a few advanced recipes on connecting two networks and handling traffic to websites.

Chapter 4, *Security*, discusses how to use some out-of-the-box security tools provided by the GCP and how GCP provides APIs to set up your own security systems.

Chapter 5, *Machine Learning and Big Data*, contains a few recipes that show the breadth of the big data offerings of GCP and some applied machine learning APIs, which will be directly consumed for our needs.

Chapter 6, *Management Tools*, shows us some recipes on the Stackdriver suite and the logging system to help us manage our Cloud Platform.

Chapter 7, *Best Practices*, covers some third-party tools and processes that can be used at the enterprise scale to derive the maximum benefit from the GCP.

To get the most out of this book

The readers should have a Linux VM, which is where the examples can be downloaded to and executed. The Linux VM will act as your development machine. Make sure that your development machine has enough space to handle the number of dependencies that will be installed along with the code. A basic understanding of cloud services and GCP is necessary.

Few recipes have simple configuration of services and others will require changes to source code. Hence, a familiarity with a programming language (Python/Node.js) and basic Linux knowledge will be beneficial.

Due to the rapid evolution of tools and dependencies, there is the possibility of commands and code breaking. Head over to the documentation if you need to modify the commands/code to suit your needs.

Download the example code files

You can download the example code files for this book from your account at www.packtpub.com. If you purchased this book elsewhere, you can visit www.packtpub.com/support and register to have the files emailed directly to you.

You can download the code files by following these steps:

1. Log in or register at www.packtpub.com.
2. Select the **SUPPORT** tab.
3. Click on **Code Downloads & Errata**.
4. Enter the name of the book in the **Search** box and follow the onscreen instructions.

Once the file is downloaded, please make sure that you unzip or extract the folder using the latest version of:

- WinRAR/7-Zip for Windows
- Zipeg/iZip/UnRarX for Mac
- 7-Zip/PeaZip for Linux

The code bundle for the book is also hosted on GitHub at https://github.com/PacktPublishing/Google-Cloud-Platform-Cookbook. In case there's an update to the code, it will be updated on the existing GitHub repository.

We also have other code bundles from our rich catalog of books and videos available at https://github.com/PacktPublishing/. Check them out!

Download the color images

We also provide a PDF file that has color images of the screenshots/diagrams used in this book. You can download it here: https://www.packtpub.com/sites/default/files/downloads/GoogleCloudPlatformCookbook_ColorImages.pdf.

Conventions used

There are a number of text conventions used throughout this book.

CodeInText: Indicates code words in text, database table names, folder names, filenames, file extensions, pathnames, dummy URLs, user input, and Twitter handles. Here is an example: "In the alpha-mgmt network, open the SSH port 22 to all servers with the network tag alpha-server."

A block of code is set as follows:

```
#! /bin/bash
apt-get update
apt-get install -y apache2
cat <<EOF > /var/www/html/index.html
<html><body><h1>Hello World</h1>
<p>Web server on the alpha and beta networks</p>
</body></html>
EOF
```

When we wish to draw your attention to a particular part of a code block, the relevant lines or items are set in bold:

```
### Hardcoding tokens in a program is never a good idea. This can be
used only for learning ###
access_token = ""
access_token_secret = ""
consumer_key = ""
consumer_secret = ""
```

Any command-line input or output is written as follows:

```
$ sudo echo "1 rt1" >> /etc/iproute2/rt_tables
```

Bold: Indicates a new term, an important word, or words that you see onscreen. For example, words in menus or dialog boxes appear in the text like this. Here is an example: "Choose the **Automatic** option under **Subnet creation mode**."

Warnings or important notes appear like this.

Tips and tricks appear like this.

Sections

In this book, you will find several headings that appear frequently (*Getting ready, How to do it..., How it works..., There's more...,* and *See also*).

To give clear instructions on how to complete a recipe, use these sections as follows:

Getting ready

This section tells you what to expect in the recipe and describes how to set up any software or any preliminary settings required for the recipe.

How to do it...

This section contains the steps required to follow the recipe.

How it works...

This section usually consists of a detailed explanation of what happened in the previous section.

There's more...

This section consists of additional information about the recipe in order to make you more knowledgeable about the recipe.

See also

This section provides helpful links to other useful information for the recipe.

Get in touch

Feedback from our readers is always welcome.

General feedback: Email `feedback@packtpub.com` and mention the book title in the subject of your message. If you have questions about any aspect of this book, please email us at `questions@packtpub.com`.

Errata: Although we have taken every care to ensure the accuracy of our content, mistakes do happen. If you have found a mistake in this book, we would be grateful if you would report this to us. Please visit www.packtpub.com/submit-errata, selecting your book, clicking on the Errata Submission Form link, and entering the details.

Piracy: If you come across any illegal copies of our works in any form on the internet, we would be grateful if you would provide us with the location address or website name. Please contact us at copyright@packtpub.com with a link to the material.

If you are interested in becoming an author: If there is a topic that you have expertise in and you are interested in either writing or contributing to a book, please visit authors.packtpub.com.

Reviews

Please leave a review. Once you have read and used this book, why not leave a review on the site that you purchased it from? Potential readers can then see and use your unbiased opinion to make purchase decisions, we at Packt can understand what you think about our products, and our authors can see your feedback on their book. Thank you!

For more information about Packt, please visit packtpub.com.

1
Compute

In this chapter, we will cover the following topics:

- Hosting a Node.js application on Google Compute Engine
- Hosting the Node.js application on Google App Engine
- Hosting a Node.js application on Kubernetes Engine
- Hosting an application on Google Cloud Functions
- Hosting a highly scalable application on Google Compute Engine

Introduction

Google provides four options for the computing needs of your application. Compute Engine gives us the option to run VMs on Google Cloud Platform's infrastructure. It also provides all the networking and security features needed to run **infrastructure as a service (IaaS)** workloads. Google App Engine is a **platform as a service** (**PaaS**) offering that supports most of the major programming languages. It comes in two flavors, a standard environment based on container instances and a flexible environment based on Compute Engine. Google Kubernetes Engine offers a Kubernetes-powered container platform for all containerized applications. Finally, for all serverless application needs, Google Cloud Functions provides the compute power and integration with other cloud services.

Hosting a Node.js application on Google Compute Engine

We'll implement a Node.js application (http://keystonejs.com/) on **Google Compute Engine (GCE)**. GCE is Google's offering for all IaaS needs. Our simple application is built on expressjs and MongoDB. expressjs is a simple web application framework for Node.js and MongoDB is a document-oriented NoSQL database. KeystoneJS also uses a templating engine along with Node.js and MongoDB.

The architecture of our recipe is depicted as follows:

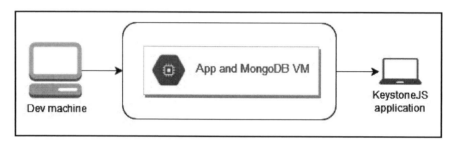

Single-tiered Node.js application on GCE

We will follow a single-tiered approach to host the application and the database on the same VM. Later in this chapter, we'll host the same Node.js application on Google App Engine and Kubernetes Engine.

You'll be using the following services and others for this recipe:

- GCE
- Google Cloud logging
- Google Cloud Source Repositories

Getting ready

The following are the initial setup verification steps to be taken before the recipe can be executed:

1. Create or select a GCP project.
2. Enable billing and enable the default APIs (some APIs such as BigQuery, storage, monitoring, and a few others are enabled automatically).
3. Install Google Cloud SDK on your development machine. Please follow the steps from `https://cloud.google.com/sdk/docs/`.
4. Install Node.js and MongoDB on your development machine.

How to do it...

We'll approach this recipe in two stages. In the first stage, we'll prepare our development machine to run our sample Node.js application. Then we'll push the working application to the Compute Engine.

Running the application on the development machine

Follow these steps to download the source code from GitHub and configure it to work on your development machine:

1. Clone the repository in your development space:

   ```
   $ git clone https://github.com/legorie/gcpcookbook.git
   ```

   You can also download the code from: `https://github.com/PacktPublishing/Google-Cloud-Platform-Cookbook`.

2. Navigate to the directory where the `mysite` application is stored:

   ```
   $ cd gcpcookbook/Chapter01/mysite
   ```

3. With your favorite editor, create a filename .env in the mysite folder:

```
COOKIE_SECRET=d44d5c45e7f8149aabc068244
MONGO_URI=mongodb://localhost/mysite
```

4. Install all the packages required for the application to work:

```
$ npm install
```

5. Start the mongod service in your development machine

6. Run the application:

```
$ node keystone.js
```

7. You'll see the following message logged on the Terminal:

```
-------------------------------------------------
Applying update 0.0.1-admins...


-------------------------------------------------
mySite: Successfully applied update 0.0.1-admins.

Successfully created:

* 1 User


-------------------------------------------------
Successfully applied 1 update.
-------------------------------------------------


-------------------------------------------------
KeystoneJS Started:
mySite is ready on port 3000
-------------------------------------------------
```

8. The application is now available on `http://localhost:3000`, as shown:

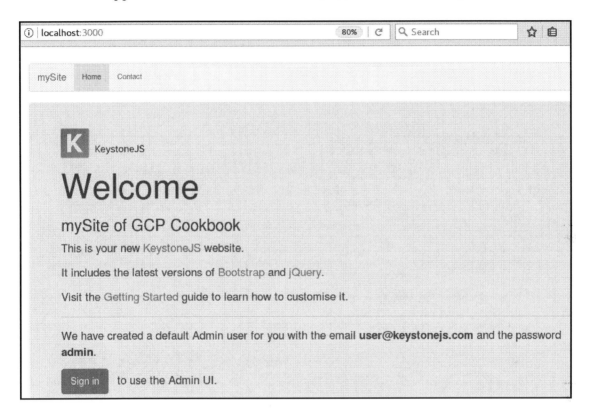

9. You can stop the local server by pressing *Ctrl + C*.

Deploying the application on GCP

To deploy the application to GCP, we'll first upload the working code from our development machine to Google Source Repositories. Then, instead of setting up the VM manually, we'll modify and use a start up script provided by Google to bootstrap the VM with the necessary packages and a runnable application. Finally, we'll create the VM with the bootstrap script and configure the firewall rules so that the application is accessible from the internet.

Moving the code to Google Source Repositories

Each project on GCP has a Git repository which can be accessed by the GCE instances. Though we can manually move the code to an instance, moving it to Source Repositories gives the ability for the compute instances to pull the code automatically via a start up script:

1. If you have made any changes to the code, you can commit the code to the local repository:

   ```
   git commit -am "Ready to be committed to GCP"
   ```

2. Create a new repository under the project:

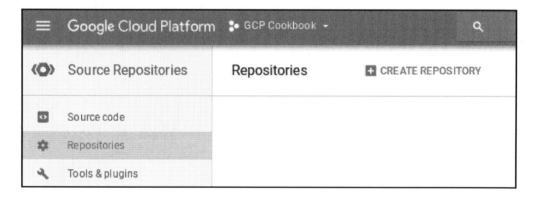

3. Follow the steps to upload the code from the local repository to Google Source Repositories. In the following example, the project ID is `gcp-cookbook` and the repository name is `gcpcookbook`:

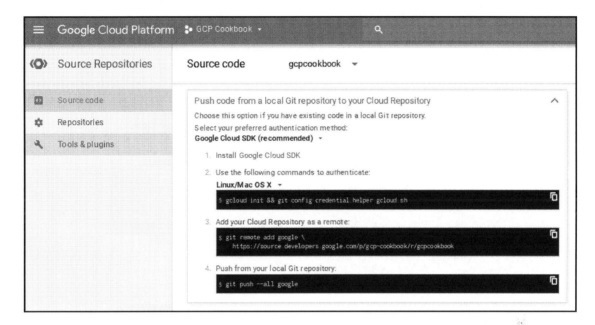

4. After the `git push` command is successful, you'll see the repository updated in the Source Repositories:

Creating the start up script

The start up script is used to initialize the VM during a boot or a restart with the necessary software (MongoDB, Node.js, supervisor, and others) and loads the application from the source code repository. The following script can be found in the `/Chapter01/` folder of the Git repository. The start up script performs the following tasks:

1. Installs the logging agent which is an application based on Fluentd.
2. Installs the MongoDB database to be used by the KeystoneJS application.
3. Installs Node.js, Git, and supervisor. Supervisor is a process control system which is used to run our KeystoneJS application as a process.
4. Clones the application code from the repository to the local folder. Update the code at `#Line 60`, to reflect your repository's URL:

   ```
   git clone https://source.developers.google.com/p/<PROJECT
   ID>/r/<REPOSITORY NAME> /opt/app #Line 60
   ```

5. Installs the dependencies and creates the `.env` file to hold the environment variables:

   ```
   COOKIE_SECRET=<Long Random String>
   ```

6. The application is configured to run under the supervisor:

   ```
   #! /bin/bash
   # Source url:
   https://github.com/GoogleCloudPlatform/nodejs-getting-started/blob/
   master/7-gce/gce/startup-script.sh
   # The startup-script is modified to suit the Chapter 01-Recipe 01
   of our book
   #  Copyright 2017, Google, Inc.
   # Licensed under the Apache License, Version 2.0 (the "License");
   # you may not use this file except in compliance with the License.
   # You may obtain a copy of the License at
   #
   #    http://www.apache.org/licenses/LICENSE-2.0
   #
   # Unless required by applicable law or agreed to in writing,
   software
   # distributed under the License is distributed on an "AS IS" BASIS,
   # WITHOUT WARRANTIES OR CONDITIONS OF ANY KIND, either express or
   implied.
   # See the License for the specific language governing permissions
   and
   # limitations under the License.
   ```

```
# [START startup]
set -v
```

7. Talks to the metadata server to get the project ID:

```
PROJECTID=$(curl -s
"http://metadata.google.internal/computeMetadata/v1/project/project
-id" -H "Metadata-Flavor: Google")
# Install logging monitor. The monitor will automatically pick up
logs sent to
# syslog.
# [START logging]
curl -s
"https://storage.googleapis.com/signals-agents/logging/google-fluen
td-install.sh" | bash
service google-fluentd restart &
# [END logging]
```

8. Installs MongoDB:

```
apt-key adv --keyserver hkp://keyserver.ubuntu.com:80 --recv
EA312927
echo "deb http://repo.mongodb.org/apt/ubuntu xenial/mongodb-org/3.2
multiverse" | sudo tee /etc/apt/sources.list.d/mongodb-org-3.2.list
apt-get update
apt-get install -y mongodb-org
cat > /etc/systemd/system/mongodb.service << EOF
[Unit]
Description=High-performance, schema-free document-oriented
database
After=network.target
[Service]
User=mongodb
ExecStart=/usr/bin/mongod --quiet --config /etc/mongod.conf
[Install]
WantedBy=multi-user.target
EOF
systemctl start mongodb
systemctl enable mongodb
```

9. Installs dependencies from apt:

```
apt-get install -yq ca-certificates git nodejs build-essential
supervisor
```

10. Installs Node.js:

```
mkdir /opt/nodejs
curl https://nodejs.org/dist/v4.2.2/node-v4.2.2-linux-x64.tar.gz |
tar xvzf - -C /opt/nodejs --strip-components=1
ln -s /opt/nodejs/bin/node /usr/bin/node
ln -s /opt/nodejs/bin/npm /usr/bin/npm
```

11. Gets the application source code from the Google Cloud Source Repositories:

```
# git requires $HOME and it's not set during the startup script.
export HOME=/root
git config --global credential.helper gcloud.sh
git clone https://source.developers.google.com/p/<Project
ID>/r/gcpcookbook   /opt/app
```

12. Installs the app dependencies:

```
cd /opt/app/Chapter01/mysite
npm install
cat >./.env << EOF
COOKIE_SECRET=d44d5c45e7f8149aabc06a830dba5716b4bd952a639c82499954
MONGODB_URI=mongodb://localhost:27017
EOF
```

13. Creates a nodeapp user. The application will run as this user:

```
useradd -m -d /home/nodeapp nodeapp
chown -R nodeapp:nodeapp /opt/app
```

14. Configures the supervisor to run the nodeapp:

```
cat >/etc/supervisor/conf.d/node-app.conf << EOF
[program:nodeapp]
directory=/opt/app/Chapter01/mysite
command=npm start
autostart=true
autorestart=true
user=nodeapp
environment=HOME="/home/nodeapp",USER="nodeapp",NODE_ENV="productio
n"
stdout_logfile=syslog
stderr_logfile=syslog
EOF
supervisorctl reread
```

```
supervisorctl update
# Application should now be running under supervisor
# [END startup]
```

Creating and configuring a GCE instance

After creating the start up script, follow these steps:

1. With the start up script ready, we can create an instance using the `gcloud` command:

```
$ gcloud compute instances create mysite-instance \
--image-family=debian-8 \
--image-project=debian-cloud \
--machine-type=g1-small \
--scopes userinfo-email,cloud-platform \
--metadata-from-file startup-script=./startup-script.sh \
--zone us-east1-c \
--tags mysite-server
```

2. You can check the progress of the instance creation using the following command:

```
$ gcloud compute instances get-serial-port-output \
mysite-instance --zone us-east1-c
```

3. Create a firewall rule to allow access to port 3000 to the instance:

```
$ gcloud compute firewall-rules create default-allow-http-3000 \
--allow tcp:3000 \
--source-ranges 0.0.0.0/0 \
--target-tags mysite-server \
--description "Allow port 3000 access to mysite-server"
```

The following screenshot shows the details of the firewall rule:

The tags on the firewall rule and the create instance commands should match.

4. Get the public IP of the instance from the Google Cloud Console or by using the following command:

```
$ gcloud compute instances list
```

5. Navigate to `http://<public IP of the instance>:3000` to see the application running.

Hosting the Node.js application on Google App Engine

We'll implement the same Node.js application used in the first recipe on Google App Engine. App Engine is a PaaS solution where we just need to deploy the code in any of the supported languages (Node.js, Java, Ruby, C#, Go, Python, and PHP), and the platform takes care of scaling automatically, health checking, and updates to the underlying OS.

App Engine provides the compute power for the application and so for the database, we'll have to use a managed MongoDB service such as mLab or a MongoDB instance of GCE. As we already have a VM running MongoDB from our previous recipe, we'll use that to serve our application running on App Engine.

Getting ready

The following are the initial setup verification steps to be taken before the recipe can be executed:

1. Create or select a GCP project.
2. Enable billing and enable the default APIs (some APIs such as BigQuery, storage, monitoring, and a few others are enabled automatically).
3. Verify that Google Cloud SDK is installed on your development machine.
4. Verify that the default project is set properly:

    ```
    $ gcloud config list
    ```

5. The VM which runs MongoDB from our first recipe allows connections only from the localhost. We'll have to modify the configuration to allow connections from the external world.
6. SSH into the VM from the Console:

7. Navigate to the MongoDB's configuration file, `/etc/mongod.conf`, and update the `bindIp` value to include `0.0.0.0`:

    ```
    # network interfaces
    net:
    ```

```
port: 27017
bindIp: [127.0.0.1,0.0.0.0]
```

In a few versions of Mongo, it is just enough to comment our the `bind_ip` line in the `mongodb` config to allow access from outside the instance.

8. Reboot the machine and verify that the MongoDB service is up and running.
9. We'll also create a new firewall rule to allow access to port `27017` from anywhere:

```
$ gcloud compute firewall-rules \
create default-allow-mongo-27017 \
--allow tcp:27017 \
--source-ranges 0.0.0.0/0 \
--target-tags mysite-server \
--description "Allow port 27017 access to mysite-server"
```

The following screenshot shows the details of the firewall rule:

The MongoDB instance is now open to the world without any login credentials. So for production systems, make sure you secure the MongoDB instance with an admin user and run the `mongod` process using the `--auth` option.

10. Connect to the MongoDB instance running on the VM from your development machine:

```
$ mongo mongodb://<External IP>:27017
```

How to do it...

With the MongoDB server up and running, we'll make a few configurational changes and deploy the application to the App Engine:

1. Logging into the Cloud Platform Console, create an App Engine application, select the region where the application will be hosted and enable billing. You can follow along with the interactive tutorial provided by Google to host your first Node.js application to the App Engine.

2. In the development machine, copy the `Chapter01/mysite` folder to a new folder called `Chapter01/mysite-ae` from where we'll push the code to the App Engine:

```
$ cp mysite/ mysite-ae/ -r
```

3. Navigate to the `mysite-ae` folder. Open the `.env` file and update the path for `MONGO_URI` to point to our VM:

```
MONGO_URI=mongodb://<External IP>:27017/mysite
```

4. Verify that all the packages are installed and launch the application on the development machine, pointing to the database on the Cloud:

```
$ npm install
$ npm start
```

5. The application's configurations are governed by a file called app.yaml. Create a new file with the following content:

```
# Basic configurations for the NodeJS application
runtime: nodejs
env: flex
```

6. Now, we can deploy the application to the App Engine:

```
$ gcloud app deploy
```

7. Once the application is deployed, the URL to access the application is provided. Fire up your favorite browser and navigate to the appspot URL and verify that the KeystoneJS application is running properly:

```
.....
5cbd6acfb] to complete...done.
Updating service [default]...done.
Deployed service [default] to [https://<project-id>.appspot.com]
```

8. You can stream logs from the command line by running:

```
$ gcloud app logs tail -s default
```

9. To view your application in the web browser run:

```
$ gcloud app browse
```

Hosting a Node.js application on Kubernetes Engine

We will containerize the KeystoneJS application and host it on **Google Kubernetes Engine (GKE)**. GKE is powered by the container management system, Kubernetes. Containers are built to do one specific task, and so we'll separate the application and the database as we did for App Engine.

The MongoDB container will host the MongoDB database with the data stored on external disks. The data within a container is transient, and so we need an external disk to safely store the MongoDB data. The App Container includes a Node.js runtime, that will run our KeystoneJS application.

It will communicate with the Mongo Container and also expose itself to the end user:

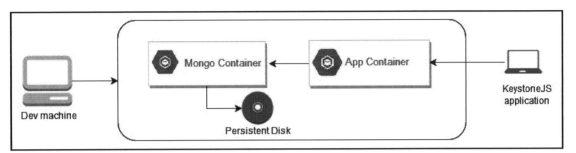

You'll be using the following services and others for this recipe:

- Google Kubernetes Engine
- GCE
- Google Container Registry

Getting ready

The following are the initial setup verification steps to be taken before the recipe can be executed:

1. Create or select a GCP project.
2. Enable billing and enable the default APIs (some APIs such as BigQuery, storage, monitoring, and a few others are enabled automatically).
3. Verify that Google Cloud SDK is installed on your development machine.
4. Verify that the default project is set properly.
5. Install Docker on your development machine.
6. Install `kubectl`, the command-line tool for running commands against Kubernetes clusters:

```
$ gcloud components install kubectl
```

How to do it...

The steps involved are:

1. Creating a cluster on GKE to host the containers
2. Containerizing the KeystoneJS application
3. Creating a replicated deployment for the application and MongoDB
4. Creating a load-balanced service to route traffic to the deployed application

Creating a cluster on GKE to host the containers

The container engine cluster runs on top of GCE. For this recipe, we'll create a two-node cluster which will be internally managed by Kubernetes:

1. We'll create the cluster using the following command:

   ```
   $ gcloud container clusters create mysite-cluster
     --scopes "cloud-platform" --num-nodes 2 --zone us-east1-c
   ```

   The gcloud command automatically generates a kubeconfig entry that enables us to use kubectl on the cluster:

2. Using kubectl, verify that you have access to the created cluster:

   ```
   $ kubectl get nodes
   ```

   The gcloud command is used to manage resources on Google Cloud Project and kubectl is used to manage resources on the Container Engine/Kubernetes cluster.

Containerizing the KeystoneJS application

Follow these steps:

1. Clone the repository in your development space:

    $ git clone https://github.com/legorie/gcpcookbook.git

2. Navigate to the directory where the mysite application is stored:

    $ cd gcpcookbook/Chapter01/mysite-gke

3. With your favorite editor, create a filename .env in the mysite folder:

    ```
    PORT=8080
    COOKIE_SECRET=<a very long string>
    MONGO_URI=mongodb://mongo/mysite
    ```

    A custom port of 8080 is used for the KeystoneJS application. This port will be mapped to port 80 later in the Kubernetes service configuration. Similarly, mongo will be the name of the load-balanced MongoDB service that will be created later.

4. The Dockerfile in the folder is used to create the application's Docker image. First, it pulls a Node.js image from the registry, then it copies the application code into the container, installs the dependencies, and starts the application. Navigate to /Chapter01/mysite-gke/Dockerfile:

    ```
    #
    https://github.com/GoogleCloudPlatform/nodejs-getting-started/blob/
    master/optional-container-engine/Dockerfile
    # Dockerfile extending the generic Node image with application
    files for a
    # single application.
    FROM gcr.io/google_appengine/nodejs
    # Check to see if the version included in the base runtime
    satisfies
    # '>=0.12.7', if not then do an npm install of the latest available
    # version that satisfies it.
    RUN /usr/local/bin/install_node '>=0.12.7'
    COPY . /app/
    # You have to specify "--unsafe-perm" with npm install
    # when running as root.  Failing to do this can cause
    # install to appear to succeed even if a preinstall
    # script fails, and may have other adverse consequences
    # as well.
    # This command will also cat the npm-debug.log file after the
    # build, if it exists.
    ```

```
RUN npm install --unsafe-perm || \
  ((if [ -f npm-debug.log ]; then \
      cat npm-debug.log; \
    fi) && false)
CMD npm start
```

5. The `.dockerignore` file contains the file paths which will not be included in the Docker container.

6. Build the Docker image:

   $ docker build -t gcr.io/<Project ID>/mysite .

   Troubleshooting:

   - Error: Cannot connect to the Docker daemon. Is the Docker daemon running on this host?
   - Solution: Add the current user to the Docker group and restart the shell. Create a new Docker group if needed.

7. You can list the created Docker image:

   $ docker images

8. Push the created image to Google Container Registry so that our cluster can access this image:

   $ gcloud docker --push gcr.io/<Project ID>/mysite

Creating a replicated deployment for the application and MongoDB

Follow these steps:

1. To create an external disk, we'll use the following command:

   **$ gcloud compute disks create --size 1GB mongo-disk \
   --zone us-east1-c**

2. We'll first create the MongoDB deployment because the application expects the database's presence. A deployment object creates the desired number of pods indicated by our replica count. Notice the label given to the pods that are created. The Kubernetes system manages the pods, the deployment, and their linking to their corresponding services via label selectors. Navigate to /Chapter01/mysite-gke/db-deployment.yml:

```
apiVersion: apps/v1beta1
kind: Deployment
metadata:
  name: mongo-deployment
spec:
  replicas: 1
  template:
    metadata:
      labels:
        name: mongo
    spec:
      containers:
      - image: mongo
        name: mongo
        ports:
        - name: mongo
          containerPort: 27017
          hostPort: 27017
        volumeMounts:
          - name: mongo-persistent-storage
            mountPath: /data/db
      volumes:
        - name: mongo-persistent-storage
          gcePersistentDisk:
            pdName: mongo-disk #The created disk name
            fsType: ext4
```

 You can refer to the following link for more information on Kubernetes objects: https://kubernetes.io/docs/user-guide/walkthrough/k8s201/.

3. Use kubectl to deploy the deployment to the cluster:

```
$ kubectl create -f db-deployment.yml
```

4. You can view the deployments using the command:

```
$ kubectl get deployments
```

5. The pods created by the deployment can be viewed using the command:

```
$ kubectl get pods
```

6. To present the MongoDB pods to the application layer, we'll need to create a service. A service exposes a single static IP address to the underlying set of pods. Navigate to /Chapter01/mysite-gke/db-service.yml:

```
apiVersion: v1
kind: Service
metadata:
 labels:
   name: mongo
 name: mongo
spec:
 ports:
   - port: 27017
     targetPort: 27017
 selector:
 name: mongo #The key-value pair is matched with the label on the
 deployment
```

7. The kubectl command to create a service is:

```
$ kubectl create -f db-service.yml
```

8. You can view the status of the creation using the commands:

```
$ kubectl get services
$ kubectl describe service mongo
```

9. We'll repeat the same process for the Node.js application. For the deployment, we'll choose to have two replicas of the application pod to serve the web requests. Navigate to /Chapter01/mysite-gke/web-deployment.yml and update the <Project ID> in the image item:

```
apiVersion: apps/v1beta1
kind: Deployment
metadata:
  name: mysite-app
  labels:
    name: mysite
spec:
```

```
replicas: 2
template:
  metadata:
    labels:
      name: mysite
  spec:
    containers:
    - image: gcr.io/<Project ID>/mysite
      name: mysite
      ports:
      - name: http-server
containerPort: 8080 #KeystoneJS app is exposed on port 8080
```

10. Use `kubectl` to create the deployment:

    $ kubectl create -f web-deployment.yml

11. Finally, we'll create the service to manage the application pods. Navigate to /Chapter01/mysite-gke/web-service.yml:

```
apiVersion: v1
kind: Service
metadata:
 name: mysite
 labels:
   name: mysite
spec:
 type: LoadBalancer
 ports:
   - port: 80 #The application is exposed to the external world on
port 80
     targetPort: http-server
     protocol: TCP
 selector:
name: mysite
```

To create the service execute the below command:

$ kubectl create -f web-service.yml

12. Get the external IP of the `mysite` service and open it in a browser to view the application:

```
$ kubectl get services

NAME        CLUSTER-IP    EXTERNAL-IP      PORT(S)        AGE
kubernetes  10.27.240.1     <none>         443/TCP        49m
mongo       10.27.246.117   <none>         27017/TCP      30m
mysite      10.27.240.33  1x4.1x3.38.164 80:30414/TCP     2m
```

After the service is created, the External IP will be unavailable for a short period; you can retry after a few seconds. The Google Cloud Console has a rich interface to view the cluster components, in addition to the Kubernetes dashboard. In case of any errors, you can view the logs and verify the configurations on the Console. The **Workloads** submenu of GKE provides details of **Deployments**, the **Discovery & load balancing** submenu gives us all the services created.

Hosting an application on Google Cloud Functions

Google Cloud Functions is the serverless compute service that runs our code in response to events. The resources needed to run the code are automatically managed and scaled. At the time of writing this recipe, Google Cloud Functions is in beta. The functions can be written in JavaScript on a Node.js runtime. The functions can be invoked with an HTTP trigger, file events on Cloud Storage buckets, and messages on Cloud Pub/Sub topic.

We'll create a simple calculator using an HTTP trigger that will take the input parameters via the HTTP POST method and provide the result.

Getting ready

The following are the initial setup verification steps to be taken before the recipe can be executed:

1. Create or select a GCP project
2. Enable billing and enable the default APIs (some APIs such as BigQuery, storage, monitoring, and a few others are enabled automatically)

3. Verify that Google Cloud SDK is installed on your development machine
4. Verify that the default project is set properly

How to do it...

We'll use the simple calculator JavaScript code available on the book's GitHub repository and deploy it to Cloud Functions:

1. Navigate to the /Chapter01/calculator folder. The application code is present in index.js and the dependencies in the package.json file. As there are no dependencies for this function, the package.json file is a basic skeleton needed for the deployment.

2. The main function receives the input via the request object, validates the inputs and performs the calculation. The calculated result is then sent back to the requester via the response object and an appropriate HTTP status code. In the following code, the switch statement does the core processing of the calculator, do spend some time on it to understand the gist of this function:

```
/**
 * Responds to any HTTP request that provides the below JSON
   message in the body.
 * # Example input JSON : {"number1": 1, "operand": "mul",
   "number2": 2 }
 * @param {!Object} req Cloud Function request context.
 * @param {!Object} res Cloud Function response context.
 */
exports.calculator = function calculator(req, res) {
    if (req.body.operand === undefined) {
        res.status(400).send('No operand defined!');
    }
    else {
        // Everything is okay
        console.log("Received number1", req.body.number1);
        console.log("Received operand", req.body.operand);
        console.log("Received number2", req.body.number2);
        var error, result;
        if (isNaN(req.body.number1) || isNaN(req.body.number2)) {
            console.error("Invalid Numbers"); // different logging
            error = "Invalid Numbers!";
            res.status(400).send(error);
        }
        switch(req.body.operand)
        {
```

```
            case "+":
            case "add":
                result = req.body.number1 + req.body.number2;
                break;
            case "-":
            case "sub":
                result = req.body.number1 - req.body.number2;
                break;
            case "*":
            case "mul":
                result = req.body.number1 * req.body.number2;
                break;
            case "/":
            case "div":
                if(req.body.number2 === 0){
                    console.error("The divisor cannot be 0");
                    error = "The divisor cannot be 0";
                    res.status(400).send(error);
                }
                else{
                    result = req.body.number1/req.body.number2;
                }
                break;
            default:
                res.status(400).send("Invalid operand");
                break;
        }
        console.log("The Result is: " + result);
        res.status(200).send('The result is: ' + result);
    }
};
```

3. We'll deploy the calculator function using the following command:

```
$ gcloud beta functions deploy calculator --trigger-http
```

The entry point for the function will be automatically taken as the calculator function. If you choose to use another name, index.js, the deploy command should be updated appropriately:

4. You can test the function via the Console, your favorite API testing apps such as Postman or via the following `curl` command. The endpoint for the function can be found under the **Triggering event** tab in the Console or it will be provided after the `deploy` command:

```
Input JSON : {"number1": 1, "operand": "mul", "number2": 2 }
$ curl -X POST
https://us-central1-<ProjectID>.cloudfunctions.net/calculator
-d '{"number1": 1, "operand": "mul", "number2": 2 }'
-H "Content-Type: application/json"
The result is: 2
```

5. You can also click on the **VIEW LOGS** button in the Cloud Functions interface to view the logs of the function execution:

```
▶ ℷ  10:31:09.637  calculator  lg0mh0crh8vw  Function execution started
▶ ⓘ  10:31:09.704  calculator  lg0mh0crh8vw  Received number1 1
▶ ⓘ  10:31:09.712  calculator  lg0mh0crh8vw  Received operand mul
▶ ⓘ  10:31:09.712  calculator  lg0mh0crh8vw  Received number2 2
▶ ⓘ  10:31:09.712  calculator  lg0mh0crh8vw  The Result is: 2
▶ ℷ  10:31:09.714  calculator  lg0mh0crh8vw  Function execution took 78 ms, finished with status code: 200
```

Hosting a highly scalable application on Google Compute Engine

There are a number of ways to host a highly scalable application on GCP using Compute Engine, App Engine, and Container Engine. We'll look at a simple PHP and MySQL application hosted on GCE with Cloud SQL and see how the GCP ecosystem helps us in building it in a scalable manner.

First, we'll create a Cloud SQL instance, which will be used by the application servers. The application servers should be designed to be replicated at will depending on any events, such as CPU usage, high utilization, and so on.

So, we'll create an *instance template* which is a definition of how GCP should create a new application server when it is needed. We feed in the start up script that prepares the instance to our requirements.

Then, we create an *instance group* which is a group of identical instances defined by the instance template. The instance group also monitors the health of the instances to make sure they maintain the defined number of servers. It automatically identifies unhealthy instances and recreates them as defined by the template.

Later, we create an HTTP(S) load balancer to serve traffic to the instance group we have created. With the load balancer in place, we now have two instances serving traffic to the users under a single endpoint provided by the load balancer. Finally, to handle any unexpected load, we'll use the *autoscaling* feature of the instance group.

Getting ready

The following are the initial setup verification steps to be taken before the recipe can be executed:

1. Create or select a GCP project
2. Enable billing and enable the default APIs (some APIs such as BigQuery, storage, monitoring, and a few others are enabled automatically)
3. Enable the Google Cloud SQL API
4. Verify that Google Cloud SDK is installed on your development machine
5. Verify that the default project is set properly

How to do it...

The implementation approach would be to first create the backend service (the database), then the instance-related setup, and finally the load balancing setup:

1. Let's first create a Cloud SQL instance. On the Google Console, navigate to the **SQL** menu item under **Storage**.
2. Click on **Create instance** and select **MySQL**.
3. Choose the recommended MySQL second generation and fill out the details:

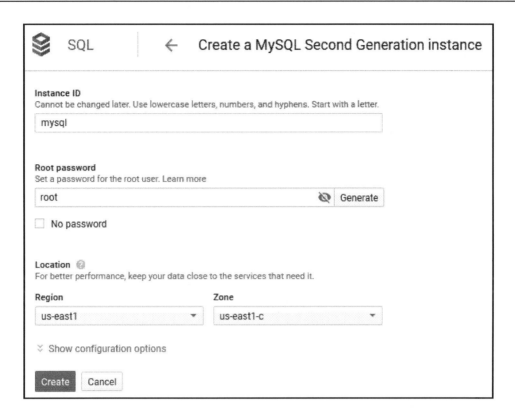

 The `root` password is set to a simple password for demonstration purposes.

4. Note the **IP address** of the Cloud SQL instance that will be fed to the configuration file in the next step:

Instance ID	Type	IP address	Instance connection name
mysql	MySQL 2nd Gen 5.7	35.190.175.176	gcp-cookbook:us-east1:mysql

5. Navigate to the `/Chapter01/php-app/pdo` folder. Edit the `config.php` file as follows:

```
$host       = "35.190.175.176" // IP Address of the Cloud SQL
$username   = "root";
$password   = "";
```

```
// Password which was given during the creation
$dbname     = "test";
$dsn        = "mysql:host=$host;dbname=$dbname";
$options    = array(
                PDO::ATTR_ERRMODE => PDO::ERRMODE_EXCEPTION
            );
```

6. The PHP application code is now ready to be hosted and replicated into multiple machines. Commit the changes to the Source Repositories from where the start up scripts will pick the code.

7. The `startup-script.sh` can be found in the `Chapter01/php-app/` directory. The script installs the necessary software to run the PHP application, then it downloads the application code from Source Repositories and moves it to the `/var/www/html` folder and installs the components for logging. Do update the project ID and the repository name in the following script to point to your GCP repository:

```
#!/bin/bash
# Modified from https://github.com/GoogleCloudPlatform/
getting-started-php/blob/master/optional-compute-engine/gce/
startup-script.sh
# [START all]
set -e
export HOME=/root
# [START php]
apt-get update
apt-get install -y git apache2 php5 php5-mysql php5-dev php-pear
pkg-config mysql-client
# Fetch the project ID from the Metadata server
PROJECTID=$(curl -s
"http://metadata.google.internal/computeMetadata/v1/project/
 project-id" -H "Metadata-Flavor: Google")
# Get the application source code
git config --global credential.helper gcloud.sh
git clone
https://source.developers.google.com/p/<Project ID>/r/<Repository
Name> /opt/src -b master
#ln -s /opt/src/optional-compute-engine /opt/app
cp /opt/src/Chapter01/php-app/pdo/* /var/www/html -r
# [END php]
systemctl restart apache2
iptables -A INPUT -i eth0 -p tcp -m tcp --dport 3306 -j ACCEPT
# [START project_config]
# Fetch the application config file from the Metadata server and
add it to the project
#curl -s
```

```
"http://metadata.google.internal/computeMetadata/v1/instance/attrib
utes/project-config" \
#  -H "Metadata-Flavor: Google" >> /opt/app/config/settings.yml
# [END project_config]
# [START logging]
# Install Fluentd
sudo curl -s
"https://storage.googleapis.com/signals-agents/logging/google-fluen
td-install.sh" | bash
# Start Fluentd
service google-fluentd restart &
# [END logging]
# [END all]
```

8. Do make sure the `firewall-rules` are updated to allow traffic for ports 80 and 3306. The instances are tagged `http-server`, so include them in the `target-tags` attribute.

9. We'll create an instance group for a group of the same PHP application servers. Create an instance template as follows:

```
$ gcloud compute instance-templates create my-php-tmpl \
--machine-type=g1-small \
--scopes logging-write,storage-ro,
https://www.googleapis.com/auth/projecthosting \
--metadata-from-file startup-script=./startup-script.sh \
--image-family=debian-8 \
--image-project=debian-cloud \
--tags http-server
```

The following screenshot shows the output for the preceding command:

Create the instance group as follows:

```
$ gcloud compute instance-groups managed create my-php-group \
--base-instance-name my-php-app \
--size 2 \
--template my-php-tmpl \
--zone us-east1-c
```

The following screenshot shows the output for the preceding command:

We'll create a health check that will poll the instance at specified intervals to verify that they can continue to serve traffic:

```
gcloud compute http-health-checks create php-health-check --
request-path /public/index.php
```

The following screenshot shows the output for the preceding command:

10. Now, we have two instances running in our instance group, my-php-group. We'll bring them under a load balancer to serve traffic.

11. Head over to the **Load balancing** submenu and let's create a new HTTP(S) load balancer by navigating to **Networking** | **Network Services** | **Load balancing**:

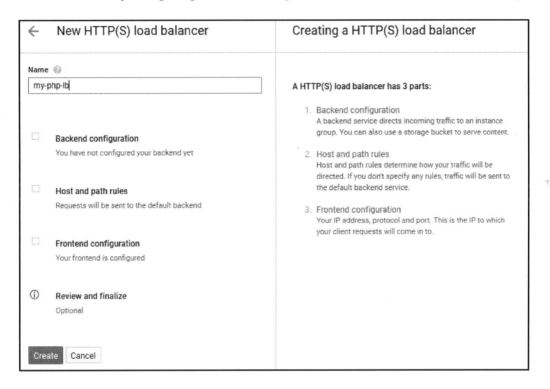

12. For the **Backend configuration,** we'll have to create a backend service which will point to the instance group and the health check that we have already created:

13. For the **Host and path rules** and **Frontend configuration**, we'll leave the default settings.

14. Once the settings are completed, an example review screen is shown as follows:

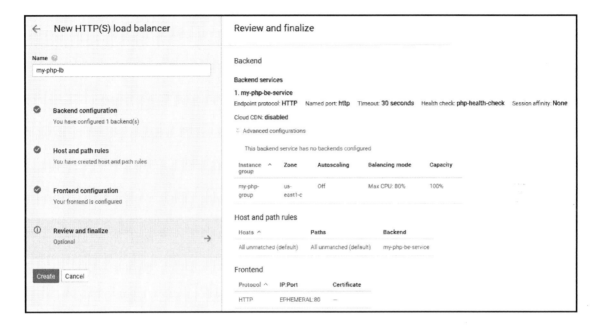

15. Go ahead and create the HTTP(S) load balancer—an external IP address is created to address the load balancer. After some time, once the instances are identified as healthy, the load balancer will serve traffic to our instances under the group:

16. In cases where traffic cannot be handled by the fixed number of instances under a load balancer, GCP provides a Compute Engine autoscaler. For scalability based on certain criteria, we can configure autoscaling at the instance group level. Instances can be scaled depending on CPU usage, HTTP load balancing usage, monitoring metrics and a combination of these factors:

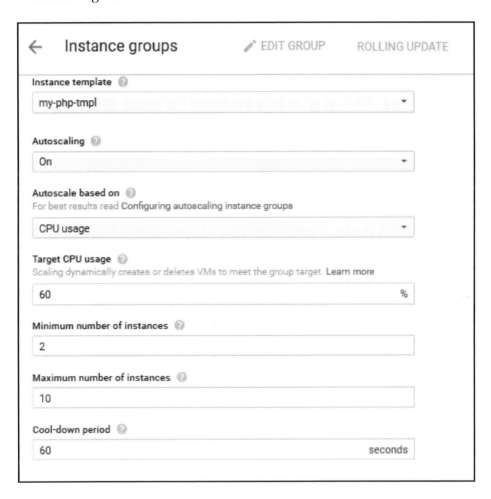

How it works...

When the user hits the endpoint URL of the load balancer, it transfers the request to one of the available instances under its control. A load balancer constantly checks for the health of the instance under its supervision. The URL to test for the health is set up using the Google Compute's health check.

The PHP applications running on both the instances are configured to use the same Cloud SQL database. So, irrespective of the request hitting **Instance 1** or **Instance 2**, the data is dealt from the common Cloud SQL database.

Also, the **Autoscaler** is turned on in the **Instance Group** governing the two instances. If there is an increase in usage (CPU in our example), the **Autoscaler** will spawn a new instance to handle the increase in traffic:

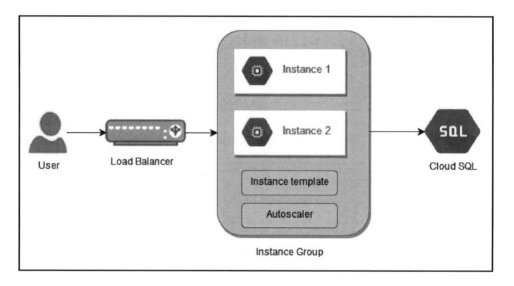

2
Storage and Databases

In this chapter, we will cover:

- Hosting a static application on Google Cloud Storage
- Image resizing using Google Cloud Storage and Cloud Functions
- Migrating a MariaDB to Cloud Spanner
- Loading temperature data to Cloud Bigtable and BigQuery-ing it
- Storage metadata in Google Cloud Datastore

Introduction

In this chapter, we'll discover some use cases for Google's Cloud Storage offerings. Storage is one of the main pillars of any workload to be hosted on **Google Cloud Platform (GCP)**. GCP offers various options for data to be stored. The nature of the data, nature of the workload, scalability and latency needs to dictate the choice of the storage. We'll cover a few examples on Google Storage, Cloud Spanner, Cloud Bigtable, BigQuery and Cloud Datastore.

In addition to Node.js, we'll use Python for a few recipes in this chapter.

 The following page is a wonderful guide for choosing a storage option for your particular workload https://cloud.google.com/storage-options/.

Hosting a static application using Google Cloud Storage

Google Storage offers a way of hosting static web applications using buckets. All client-side technologies (HTML, CSS, and JavaScript) can be hosted in a bucket. This option is very inexpensive to host and can scale to a great extent. The costs incurred will be on the assets stored, outbound network traffic and retrieval from storage. We'll use Hugo (`https://gohugo.io`), a static website generator and host the generated code in a storage bucket. In addition to hosting a static website, the static contents (CSS, JavaScript, and images) of a dynamic website hosted on Google Storage is also a widely accepted use case.

Getting ready

The following are the initial setup verification steps to be carried out before the recipe can be executed:

1. Create or select a GCP project
2. Enable billing and enable the default APIs (some APIs such as BigQuery, storage, monitoring, and a few others are enabled automatically)
3. Install the Google Cloud SDK on your development machine, we'll be using the `gsutil` command
4. Install Hugo on your development machine: `https://gohugo.io/getting-started/installing/`

How to do it...

The steps involved are as follows:

1. With Hugo successfully installed, let's create a static site. Navigate to your desired folder and use the following command:

```
hugo new site staticSite
```

2. Now, a standard folder structure and the configuration file are created for the Hugo website. By default, there are no themes installed, hence we'll use the **Ananke** theme to give our website some luster:

```
cd ./staticSite/themes
git clone https://github.com/budparr/gohugo-theme-ananke.git
```

3. The theme is downloaded in the `themes` folder. Use your favorite editor and add `theme = "gohugo-theme-ananke"` to the `config.toml` file.

4. We'll create our first post using the following command:

```
hugo new posts/first-post.md
```

 Some themes look for posts under the `post` folder, so the directory setting and configuration need to be adjusted according to the theme selected.

5. Hugo comes with a built-in web server. To view the website and the first post, run the server with the `-D` option:

```
hugo server -D
```

 The website will be available at `http://localhost:1313`.

6. To publish the first post, set the `drafts` tag to `false` in the file `staticSite/content/posts/first-post.md`. Now the web server without the `-D` flag will serve the static website.

7. Ideally the `baseURL` in the `config.toml` file will contain the base URL of our website. As we are testing the use of Google Storage for static website hosting, update the `baseURL` as follows in the `config.toml` file:

```
baseURL = "."
```

8. Once we are satisfied with the content, we can generate the static website using the `hugo` command. This command generates the `/public` folder with all the elements to host the static website.

If you are recreating the website for deployment, it is recommended you remove the `public` folder and rerun the `hugo` command.

9. In the Google Console, create a bucket to host the website. We'll create one with the name `static_site`.

10. Navigate to the `./staticSite/public` directory and push the website contents from the development machine to Google Storage:

```
gsutil cp -R * gs://static_site/
```

11. We'll also have to enable **Share publicly** to all the files in the bucket:

```
gsutil -m acl ch -r -u AllUsers:R gs://static_site/
```

12. You can now click on the publicly shareable URL of our `index.html` file to view the website: `https://storage.googleapis.com/static_site/index.html`:

There's more...

In this recipe, we have seen how to host a website without a domain name. The preceding example works best with a domain you manage or own. To make it work with your domain name, you'll have to take the following steps:

1. Name the bucket with the domain name, for example: `gs://www.example.com`.

2. Create a CNAME record pointing to `c.storage.googleapis.com`.

3. Set a website configuration for the bucket, to make it behave like a static website:

```
gsutil web set -m index.html -e 404.html gs://www.example.com
```

Reference: `https://cloud.google.com/storage/docs/hosting-static-website`.

Image resizing using Google Cloud Storage and Cloud Functions

Google Storage is extensively used to store static images to be served by different platforms. One of the needs of the modern-day digital world is to have images created for different form factors—desktop, mobile and tablet screens. In this recipe, we'll develop a Cloud Function to resize the images uploaded to a bucket:

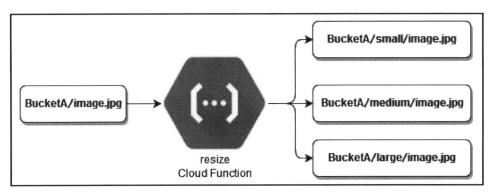

Getting ready

The following are the initial setup verification steps to be carried out before the recipe can be executed:

1. Create or select a GCP project
2. Enable billing and enable the default APIs (some APIs such as BigQuery, storage, monitoring, and a few others are enabled automatically)
3. Verify that Node.js and Google Cloud SDK are installed
4. Verify that the Google Cloud Functions API is enabled

How to do it...

The steps involved are as follows:

1. Navigate to the `Chapter02/imageresize` folder.
2. The `package.json` file contains the necessary models for our Node.js Cloud Function.
3. The `config.json` file contains the dimensions for the resizing to three different form factors.
4. The following Node.js code is triggered whenever a file is uploaded to a bucket specified during the function creation. It performs the following functions:
   - If the uploaded image is not an image, no action is performed
   - If the image name starts with `CR_`, then the file is ignored as it has already been resized by this function
   - Deletion and metadata change events are ignored
   - The image file which is to be modified is resized to three different sizes using the `sharp` module

   The following code is built in such a way as to perform all the aforementioned functions:

   ```
   'use strict';

   const storage = require('@google-cloud/storage')();
   const path = require('path');
   const sharp = require('sharp');
   const async = require('async');
   const config = require('./config.json');
   ```

```
/**
 *When an image is uploaded in the Storage bucket We generate a
 *thumbnail automatically using Sharp.
 */
exports.imageresize = function(event, callback){
  const object = event.data; // The Storage object.
  const fileBucket = object.bucket;
// The Storage bucket that contains the file.
  const filePath = object.name; // File path in the bucket.
  const contentType = object.contentType; // File content type.
  const resourceState = object.resourceState;
// The resourceState is 'exists' or 'not_exists'
// (for file/folder deletions).
  const metageneration = object.metageneration;
// Number of times metadata has been generated.
// New objects have a value of 1.
// Exit if this is triggered on a file that is not an image.
  if (!contentType.startsWith('image/')) {
    console.log('This is not an image.');
    callback();
    return;
  }
// Get the file name.
  const fileName = path.basename(filePath);
// Exit if the image is already a thumbnail.
  if (fileName.startsWith('CR_')) {
    console.log('Already resized file.');
    callback();
    return;
  }
// Exit if this is a move or deletion event.
  if (resourceState === 'not_exists') {
    console.log('This is a deletion event.');
    callback();
    return;
  }
// Exit if file exists but is not new and is only being
// triggered because of a metadata change.
  if (resourceState === 'exists' && metageneration > 1) {
    console.log('This is a metadata change event.');
    callback();
    return;
  }
// Download file from bucket.
  const bucket = storage.bucket(fileBucket);
  const metadata = {
    contentType: contentType
  };
```

```
    var itemsResized = 0;
    var config_size = Object.keys(config).length;
    console.log("config size" + config_size);
    //for (var size in config) {
    async.forEachOf(config, function (size, key, cb) {
      const MIN = size["min"];
      const MAX = size["max"];
      const size_name = size["name"];
      console.log(size_name + " " + MIN + " " + size["max"]);

// We add a 'thumb_' prefix to thumbnails file name.
// That's where we'll upload the thumbnail.
      const tempFileName = `CR_${size_name}_${fileName}`;
      const tempFilePath = path.join(path.dirname(filePath),
        size_name,tempFileName);
// Create write stream for uploading thumbnail
      const tempFileUploadStream = bucket.file(tempFilePath)
        .createWriteStream({metadata});

// Create Sharp pipeline for resizing the image and
// use pipe to read from bucket read stream
      const pipeline = sharp();
      pipeline
        .resize(MIN, MAX)
        .max()
        .pipe(tempFileUploadStream);

      bucket.file(filePath).createReadStream().pipe(pipeline);
      tempFileUploadStream.on('error', () => {
        console.log('Resize file creation failed in UploadStream');
        return cb("Resize failed");
      })
        .on('finish',() => {
          console.log('Resize file created successfully');
          cb();
          });
    },
    function (err) {
// After iterating through all the elements of the config object
      if (err) console.error(err.message);
      console.log("Done");
      callback();
      return;
    });
  };
```

5. To deploy the `resize` function, along with the `package.json` and `config.json` from the `resize` folder, issue the following command:

```
$ gcloud beta functions deploy imageresize
    --stage-bucket <some bucket>
    --trigger-bucket <bucket of the image file>
    --entry-point imageresize
```

6. You can view the uploaded function on the Console:

Name	Region	Trigger	Memory allocated	Executed function	Last deployed ∨	
⊘ imageresize	us-central1	bucket: uploadtestbuckt	256 MB	imageresize	11/23/17, 1:23 AM	⋮

7. To test the function, upload an image file into the trigger bucket and verify if three resized images are created under the `small`, `medium`, and `large` folders:

Buckets / uploadtestbuckt

Name	Size	Type	Storage class
📁 large/	—	Folder	—
📁 medium/	—	Folder	—
📁 small/	—	Folder	—

8. You can also look at the logs of the `imageresize` function to verify the successful execution.

How it works...

The serverless code (Google Function code) executes in response to an event, in this case, a Google Storage event. The Storage events are triggered whenever there is a create, update, or delete action for an object. The data of the event change is captured through the `event.data` in our code.

Migrating a MariaDB to Cloud Spanner

Google Cloud Spanner is a relational database service which is highly consistent, available and scalable horizontally. It is a fully managed service suitable for OLTP workloads and low-latency/high-throughput environments. In this recipe, we'll understand the features of Spanner in relation to a popular RDBMS, MariaDB. We'll take a simple MariaDB database and move the schema and the data to Cloud Spanner. At the time of writing, there is no automated import/export tool for Cloud Spanner, the manual method gives us a glimpse of the way Spanner is built and its strengths/weaknesses. Firstly, we'll export the data from our MariaDB database using the `mysqldump` utility. Then, we'll create the database and tables via the Google Console. Finally, we'll insert the data into the table via a Python script.

Getting ready

The following are the initial setup verification steps to be carried out before the recipe can be executed:

1. Create or select a GCP project
2. Enable billing and enable the default APIs (some APIs such as BigQuery, storage, monitoring, and a few others are enabled automatically)
3. Install the Google Cloud SDK on your development machine
4. Install Python and `pip` on your development machine

How to do it...

The steps involved are as follows:

1. A sample two-table database has been exported using the `mysqldump` utility: `https://github.com/legorie/gcpcookbook/blob/master/Chapter02/ mysql2spanner/org_extract.sql`. In the Google Console, let's create a Cloud Spanner instance for our database. In the following example, the instance created is geographically located in `us-central1`. Google replicates this instance in three availability zones within the region. With a node count of `1`, our DB instance has 2 TB of storage and can provide 10,000 **queries per sec (QPS)** for read and 2000 QPS for write:

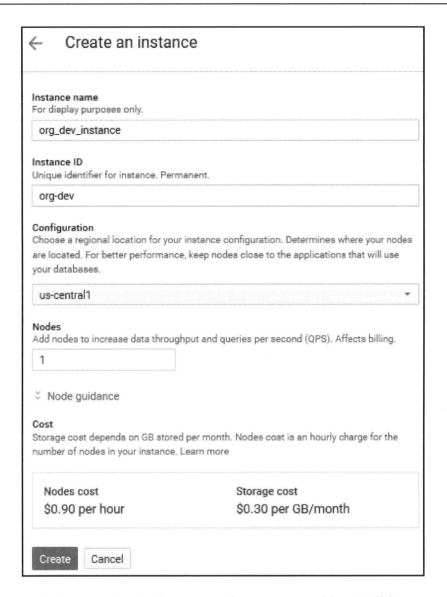

2. Next, let's create the database `org` to host our two tables. We'll first create the `offices` table as it is the child table:

```
CREATE TABLE `offices` (
  `officeCode` varchar(10) NOT NULL,
  `city` varchar(50) NOT NULL,
  `phone` varchar(50) NOT NULL,
  `addressLine1` varchar(50) NOT NULL,
```

```
   `addressLine2` varchar(50) DEFAULT NULL,
   `state` varchar(50) DEFAULT NULL,
   `country` varchar(50) NOT NULL,
   `postalCode` varchar(15) NOT NULL,
   `territory` varchar(10) NOT NULL,
   PRIMARY KEY (`officeCode`)
) ENGINE=InnoDB DEFAULT CHARSET=latin1;
```

3. To convert the DDL statement from the SQL dump to Cloud Spanner-compatible DDL, use your favorite text editor to perform the following:

   1. Remove the back quote ` from the table name and column names.

   2. Change varchar to string.

   3. Default is not supported by Cloud Spanner, we'll remove it with DEFAULT NULL.

   4. Move the PRIMARY KEY definition outside the column name definitions:

   ```
   CREATE TABLE offices (
      officeCode string(10) NOT NULL,
      city string(50) NOT NULL,
      phone string(50) NOT NULL,
      addressLine1 string(50) NOT NULL,
      addressLine2 string(50) ,
      state string(50),
      country string(50) NOT NULL,
      postalCode string(15) NOT NULL,
      territory string(10) NOT NULL
   ) PRIMARY KEY (officeCode);
   ```

4. We'll create the child table employees as follows:

   ```
   CREATE TABLE `employees` (
    `employeeNumber` int(11) NOT NULL,
    `lastName` varchar(50) NOT NULL,
    `firstName` varchar(50) NOT NULL,
    `extension` varchar(10) NOT NULL,
    `email` varchar(100) NOT NULL,
    `officeCode` varchar(10) NOT NULL,
    `reportsTo` int(11) DEFAULT NULL,
    `jobTitle` varchar(50) NOT NULL,
    PRIMARY KEY (`employeeNumber`),
    KEY `reportsTo` (`reportsTo`),
    KEY `officeCode` (`officeCode`),
    CONSTRAINT `employees_ibfk_2`
   FOREIGN KEY (`officeCode`) REFERENCES
   ```

```
`offices` (`officeCode`)
) ENGINE=InnoDB DEFAULT CHARSET=latin1;
```

The KEY attribute of the MariaDB DDL is converted into the CREATE
INDEX statement. Also, the feature similar to FOREIGN KEY is the INTERLEAVE
IN PARENT construct:

```
CREATE TABLE employees (
    officeCode string(10) NOT NULL,
    employeeNumber int64 NOT NULL,
    lastName string(50) NOT NULL,
    firstName string(50) NOT NULL,
    extension string(10) NOT NULL,
    email string(100) NOT NULL,
    reportsTo int64,
    jobTitle string(50) NOT NULL
) PRIMARY KEY (officeCode, employeeNumber),
    INTERLEAVE IN PARENT offices ON DELETE    CASCADE;

CREATE INDEX reportsTo ON employees(reportsTo);
CREATE INDEX officeCode ON employees(officeCode);
```

5. Once the tables are created, we can insert the data into the offices table using a
   Python program. As a prerequisite, we'll also have to prepare the data from the
   SQL dump to the format expected by the program: offices_dat.txt. The
   following snippet is the data from the SQL dump in the required format which
   we will be inserting into the offices table:

```
offices
('officeCode', 'city', 'phone', 'addressLine1', 'addressLine2',
'state', 'country', 'postalCode', 'territory')
(u'1',u'San Francisco',u'+1 650 219 4782',u'100 Market
Street',u'Suite 300',u'CA',u'USA',u'94080',u'NA')
(u'2',u'Boston',u'+1 215 837 0825',u'1550 Court Place',u'Suite
102',u'MA',u'USA',u'02107',u'NA')
(u'3',u'NYC',u'+1 212 555 3000',u'523 East 53rd Street',u'apt.
5A',u'NY',u'USA',u'10022',u'NA')
(u'4',u'Paris',u'+33 14 723 4404',u'43 Rue Jouffroy
D\'abbans',None,None,'France',u'75017',u'EMEA')
(u'5',u'Tokyo',u'+81 33 224 5000',u'4-1 Kioicho',None,'Chiyoda-
Ku',u'Japan',u'102-8578',u'Japan')
(u'6',u'Sydney',u'+61 2 9264 2451',u'5-11 Wentworth Avenue',u'Floor
#2',None,'Australia',u'NSW 2010',u'APAC')
(u'7',u'London',u'+44 20 7877 2041',u'25 Old Broad Street',u'Level
7',None,'UK',u'EC2N 1HN',u'EMEA')
```

The following Python code file named `insert_data2spanner.py` will read the data and insert it into the `offices` table:

```python
# Imports the Google Cloud Client Library.
from google.cloud import spanner
from ast import literal_eval as make_tuple
import sys

def insert_data(instance_id, database_id, data_file):
    """Inserts sample data into the given database.
    The database and table must already exist and can be created
using
    `create_database`.
    """
    spanner_client = spanner.Client()
    instance = spanner_client.instance(instance_id)
    database = instance.database(database_id)
    dat = []

    f = open(data_file,"r") #opens file with name of "test.txt"
    for line in f:
        dat.append(line)
    dat = [x.strip() for x in dat] # Strips newline and spaces
    table_name = dat.pop(0)
    print('Table name: ' + table_name)
    dat = [make_tuple(x) for x in dat] # Makes tuples as expected
by the insert function
    col_names = dat.pop(0)
    print('Column Names: ' + str(col_names))
    f.close()

    with database.batch() as batch:
        batch.insert(
            table=table_name,
            columns=col_names,
            values=dat)

# Instantiate a client.
spanner_client = spanner.Client()

# Your Cloud Spanner instance ID.
instance_id = 'org-dev'

# Get a Cloud Spanner instance by ID.
instance = spanner_client.instance(instance_id)

# Your Cloud Spanner database ID.
```

```
database_id = 'org'

# Get a Cloud Spanner database by ID.
database = instance.database(database_id)

data_file = sys.argv[1:].pop(0)
insert_data(instance_id, database_id, data_file)
print('Data inserted')
```

The instance and the database names are hardcoded for simplicity. Install the requirements and load the data using the following commands :

```
$ virtualenv env
$ source env/bin/activate
$ pip install -r requirements.txt
$ python insert_data2spanner.py offices_dat.txt
```

6. Similarly, after preparing the data for the `employees` table, the data can be inserted using the same program, `employees_dat.txt`:

```
employees
('employeeNumber', 'lastName', 'firstName', 'extension',
'email','officeCode', 'reportsTo','jobTitle')
(1002,u'Murphy',u'Diane',u'x5800',u'dmurphy@classicmodelcars.com',u
'1',None,u'President')
(1056,u'Patterson',u'Mary',u'x4611',u'mpatterso@classicmodelcars.co
m',u'1',1002,u'VP Sales')
(1076,u'Firrelli',u'Jeff',u'x9273',u'jfirrelli@classicmodelcars.com
',u'1',1002,u'VP Marketing')
(1088,u'Patterson',u'William',u'x4871',u'wpatterson@classicmodelcar
s.com',u'6',1056,u'Sales Manager (APAC)')
(1102,u'Bondur',u'Gerard',u'x5408',u'gbondur@classicmodelcars.com',
u'4',1056,u'Sale Manager (EMEA)')
(1143,u'Bow',u'Anthony',u'x5428',u'abow@classicmodelcars.com',u'1',
1056,u'Sales Manager (NA)')
(1165,u'Jennings',u'Leslie',u'x3291',u'ljennings@classicmodelcars.c
om',u'1',1143,u'Sales Rep')
(1166,u'Thompson',u'Leslie',u'x4065',u'lthompson@classicmodelcars.c
om',u'1',1143,u'Sales Rep')
(1188,u'Firrelli',u'Julie',u'x2173',u'jfirrelli@classicmodelcars.co
m',u'2',1143,u'Sales Rep')
(1216,u'Patterson',u'Steve',u'x4334',u'spatterson@classicmodelcars.
com',u'2',1143,u'Sales Rep')
(1286,u'Tseng',u'Foon
Yue',u'x2248',u'ftseng@classicmodelcars.com',u'3',1143,u'Sales
Rep')
(1323,u'Vanauf',u'George',u'x4102',u'gvanauf@classicmodelcars.com',
```

```
u'3',1143,u'Sales Rep')
(1337,u'Bondur',u'Loui',u'x6493',u'lbondur@classicmodelcars.com',u'
4',1102,u'Sales Rep')
(1370,u'Hernandez',u'Gerard',u'x2028',u'ghernande@classicmodelcars.
com',u'4',1102,u'Sales Rep')
(1401,u'Castillo',u'Pamela',u'x2759',u'pcastillo@classicmodelcars.c
om',u'4',1102,u'Sales Rep')
(1501,u'Bott',u'Larry',u'x2311',u'lbott@classicmodelcars.com',u'7',
1102,u'Sales Rep')
(1504,u'Jones',u'Barry',u'x102',u'bjones@classicmodelcars.com',u'7'
,1102,u'Sales Rep')
(1611,u'Fixter',u'Andy',u'x101',u'afixter@classicmodelcars.com',u'6
',1088,u'Sales Rep')
(1612,u'Marsh',u'Peter',u'x102',u'pmarsh@classicmodelcars.com',u'6'
,1088,u'Sales Rep')
(1619,u'King',u'Tom',u'x103',u'tking@classicmodelcars.com',u'6',108
8,u'Sales Rep')
(1621,u'Nishi',u'Mami',u'x101',u'mnishi@classicmodelcars.com',u'5',
1056,u'Sales Rep')
(1625,u'Kato',u'Yoshimi',u'x102',u'ykato@classicmodelcars.com',u'5'
,1621,u'Sales Rep')
(1702,u'Gerard',u'Martin',u'x2312',u'mgerard@classicmodelcars.com',
u'4',1102,u'Sales Rep')
```

You can verify the successful insertion of the data in the Console:

The following screenshot shows the detailed data of employees which was loaded using the following program:

Loading temperature data to Cloud Bigtable and BigQuery-ing it

Google Bigtable is a fully managed NoSQL service with a focus on low latency and high throughput. It is well suited for storing data for large analytical processing, operation data from IoT devices, other time-series data, and so on. Cloud Bigtable is designed for performance, for huge databases (~1 TB) and it optimizes your data over time. In this recipe, we'll have a look at a small database generated by an IoT temperature sensor. We'll write a Python script to simulate a sensor sending temperature data located in a garden to the Bigtable. Then, we'll use BigQuery to connect to the Bigtable database to query and make meaning out of the data store.

Getting ready

The following are the initial setup verification steps to be carried out before the recipe can be executed:

1. Create or select a GCP project
2. Enable billing and enable the default APIs (some APIs such as BigQuery, storage, monitoring, and a few others are enabled automatically)
3. Install the Google Cloud SDK on your development machine and set up appropriate authentication
4. Verify that the Cloud Bigtable Admin API is enabled
5. Install the command-line tools—cbt and bq
6. Install pip and virtualenv

How to do it...

The steps involved are as follows:

1. In the Console, navigate to the **Bigtable** page and click on **Create instance**.
2. Create an instance with the input data as shown in the following screenshot:

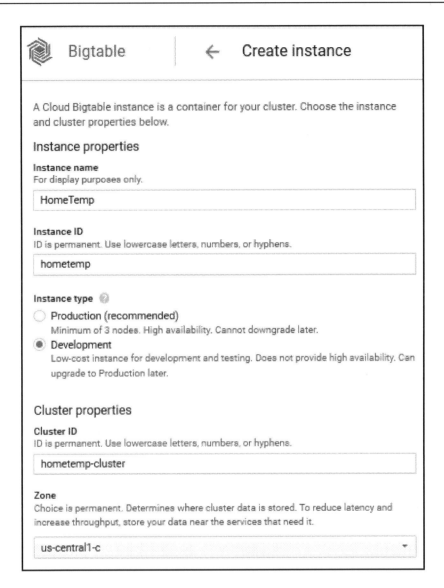

3. Clone the `bigtable` folder from the GitHub repository. The following Python script inserts sample sensor data to the Bigtable. Do update the `<Project ID>` at the last line of the `bigtableIns.py`.

Care should be taken in the schema design and how data is inserted into the Bigtable, as this will impact the performance of the Bigtable: `https://cloud.google.com/bigtable/docs/schema-design`.

The following script can be found in the `Chapter02/bigtable/bigtableIns.py` **folder:**

```python
#!/usr/bin/env python


"""Demonstrates how to connect to Cloud Bigtable and run some basic
operations.

Prerequisites:

- Create a Cloud Bigtable cluster.
  https://cloud.google.com/bigtable/docs/creating-cluster
- Set your Google Application Default Credentials.
https://developers.google.com/identity/protocols/application-defaul
t-credentials
"""

import datetime
import random
from google.cloud import bigtable

def main(project_id, instance_id, table_id):
    # [START connecting_to_bigtable]
    # The client must be created with admin=True because it will
    # create a table.
    client = bigtable.Client(project=project_id, admin=True)
    instance = client.instance(instance_id)
    # [END connecting_to_bigtable]

    # [START creating_a_table]
    print('Creating the {} table.'.format(table_id))
    table = instance.table(table_id)
    table.delete() #If you are re-running the script, the delete
table can be invoked
    #If you are re-running the script, the delete table can be
    # invoked
    table.create()
    column_family_id = 'sensorcf1'
    sensorcf1 = table.column_family(column_family_id)
    sensorcf1.create()
    # [END creating_a_table]
```

```
    # [START writing_rows]
    print('Writing sample temperature data to the table.')
    column_id = 'sensordata'.encode('utf-8')
    dt = datetime.datetime(2017, 12, 01)
    end = datetime.datetime(2017, 12, 01, 23, 59, 59)
    step = datetime.timedelta(minutes=30)

    temp = []

    while dt < end:
        temp.append(dt.strftime('%Y%m%d%H%M%S'))
        dt += step

    for i, value in enumerate(temp):
        # For more information about how to design a Bigtable
schema
        # for the best performance, see the documentation:
        #
        # https://cloud.google.com/bigtable/docs/schema-design
        row_key = 'temp'+value
        row = table.row(row_key)
    temp_data = 'GARDEN' + str(random.randint(15, 35))
        #Append a random temperature
        row.set_cell(
            column_family_id,
            column_id,
            temp_data.encode('utf-8'))
        row.commit()
    # [END writing_rows]

    # [START scanning_all_rows]
    print('Scanning for all temperature data:')
    partial_rows = table.read_rows()
    partial_rows.consume_all()

    for row_key, row in partial_rows.rows.items():
        key = row_key.decode('utf-8')
        cell = row.cells[column_family_id][column_id][0]
        value = cell.value.decode('utf-8')
        print('\t{}: {}'.format(key, value))
    # [END scanning_all_rows]

if __name__ == '__main__':
    #main(args.project_id, args.instance_id, args.table)
    main('<Project ID>','hometemp','temperature')
```

4. Create a `virtualenv` and install the dependencies:

```
$ virtualenv env
$ source env/bin/activate
$ pip install -r requirements.txt
```

5. Run the `bigtableIns.py` to insert data into the table `temperature`.

6. Now with the temperature data from the garden inserted into our table, let's find what was the highest temperature recorded on a given day. Let's head on to the **BigQuery** page and create a dataset as follows:

7. Click on **Create new table** on the `HomeTemp` dataset:

8. On the **Create Table** page:
   1. Select **Google Cloud Bigtable** for the **Location**. In the textbox, provide the Bigtable URI as follows: `https://googleapis.com/bigtable/projects/<Proje ct ID>/instances/hometemp/tables/temperature`.
   2. Enter a destination table name, for example: `temperature`.

3. The **Column Families** definition is a critical criterion for the external table mapping. Give the column family name of the Bigtable `sensorcf1`, **Type** as **STRING** and **Encoding** as **TEXT**.

4. Check the box **Read row key as string**:

9. Finally, execute the query in the query editor to get the maximum recorded temperature in the dataset:

```
SELECT
  SUBSTR(rowkey, 5) AS timestamp,
  SUBSTR(sensorcf1.column.cell.value,7) AS temperature_reading
FROM
  [<Project ID>:HomeTemp.temperature]
```

```
WHERE
  SUBSTR(sensorcf1.column.cell.value,7) = (
  SELECT
    MAX(SUBSTR(sensorcf1.column.cell.value,7))
  FROM
    [<Project ID>:HomeTemp.temperature] )
LIMIT
  1
```

10. When the preceding query is executed in the editor, we get the temperature reading as shown in the following screenshot:

Storage metadata in Google Cloud Datastore

Google Datastore is a highly scalable, NoSQL document database similar to Amazon's DynamoDB and MongoDB. Individual data objects in the Datastore are called **entities**. An entity has one or more **properties** and a category of objects is called a **kind**. Each object is uniquely identified by a **key**. In this recipe, we would simulate a storage drive environment. Employees of a company are given the ability to upload files to Google Storage. The metadata is stored in Cloud Datastore to avoid overhead to the Storage API and for efficiency. The file uploaded to the Storage follows this file format:

```
<5-digit hash>/<[year][month][day][hour][minute][second]>/<Employee
ID>/<file name>
```

After the data is uploaded to Storage, the metadata collected should enable us to query:

- List all objects uploaded by an employee
- List all objects in a time range

So, we'll design the metadata in the following format:

Kind	Drive

Entity	Data objects inserted for example:
	`[<Entity(u'Drive', 5672749318012928L) {u'filekey':`
	`'b4ef6/20171121214856/123659/requirements.txt', u'empid':`
	`'123659', u'timestamp': '20171121214856', u'created':`
	`datetime.datetime(2017, 11, 22, 2, 48, 57, 532106,`
	`tzinfo=<UTC>)}>,`

Properties	Name/ID, `created`, `empid`, `filekey`, `timestamp`
Unique ID	Name/ID

Getting ready

The following are the initial setup verification steps to be carried out before the recipe can be executed:

1. Create or select a GCP project
2. Enable billing and enable the default APIs (some APIs such as BigQuery, storage, monitoring, and a few others are enabled automatically)
3. Install the Google Cloud SDK on your development machine and set up appropriate authentication

4. Install `pip` and `virtualenv`

 The Cloud Datastore is associated with the App Engine and it should be enabled. Navigate to the Cloud Datastore and verify if it is activated.

How to do it...

The steps involved are as follows:

1. Clone the GitHub repository and navigate to the `storagedrive` directory: `https://github.com/legorie/gcpcookbook.git` or `https://github.com/PacktPublishing/Google-Cloud-Platform-Cookbook.git`.

2. Create `virtualenv` and install the dependencies to run the sample:

```
$ virtualenv env
$ source env/bin/activate
$ pip install -r requirements.txt
```

3. The Python code will upload the file specified to Google Storage and make an entry into the Cloud Datastore. We have prepended a five-digit hash to the filename so that the files are not written in a contiguous manner. This will help Google Cloud Storage better manage the auto-balancing, upload connection speed, and distribution of files. The bucket name is hardcoded in the code, so modify as per your need. The following script can be found in the `Chapter02/storagedrive/upload.py` folder:

```
import argparse
import hashlib
import datetime
from google.cloud import storage
from google.cloud import datastore

def create_client(project_id):
    return datastore.Client(project_id)

def add_drive_entry(client, gcs_filename, empid, tms):
    key = client.key('Drive')
    drive = datastore.Entity(
        key, exclude_from_indexes=['filekey'])
    drive.update({
        'created': datetime.datetime.utcnow(),
```

```python
        'filekey': gcs_filename,
        'timestamp': tms,
        'empid': empid
    })
    client.put(drive)
    return drive.key

def list_drive_entries(client):
    query = client.query(kind='Drive')
    query.order = ['created']
    return list(query.fetch())

def main(project_id, file_name):
    empid="121659"  # An hardcoded employee ID
    client = storage.Client()
    # https://console.cloud.google.com/storage/browser/[bucket-id]/
    bucket = client.get_bucket('static_site') # Hardcoded bucket id
    hash_object = hashlib.md5(file_name.encode())
    hex_dig = hash_object.hexdigest()
    gcs_filename = hex_dig[:5]
    dt = datetime.datetime.now()
    tms = dt.strftime('%Y%m%d%H%M%S')
    gcs_filename = gcs_filename + "/" + tms + "/" + empid + "/" +
file_name
    print('File name uploaded : ' + gcs_filename)
    blob2 = bucket.blob(gcs_filename)
    blob2.upload_from_filename(filename=file_name)
    ds_client = create_client(project_id)
    drive_key = add_drive_entry(ds_client, gcs_filename, empid,
tms)
    print('Task {} added.'.format(drive_key.id))
    print('=== List of entries ===')
    print(list_drive_entries(ds_client))
    print('=======================')


if __name__ == '__main__':
    parser = argparse.ArgumentParser(
    description=__doc__,
    formatter_class=argparse.ArgumentDefaultsHelpFormatter)
    parser.add_argument('project_id', help='Your Cloud Platform
project ID.')
    parser.add_argument(
    'file_name', help='Local file name')
    args = parser.parse_args()
    main(args.project_id, args.file_name)
```

4. You can upload the file running the upload program as `python upload.py`
   `<Project ID> <File to be uploaded>`:

```
(env) $ python upload.py gcp-cookbook image.jpg
File name uploaded : 0d5b1/20171121233215/121659/image.jpg
Task 5682617542246400 added.
=== List of entries ===
[<Entity(u'Drive', 5668600916475904L) {u'filekey':
'b4ef6/20171121231026/121659/requirements.txt', u'empid': '121659',
u'timestamp': '20171121231026', u'created': datetime.datetime(2017,
11, 22, 4, 10, 27, 795654, tzinfo=<UTC>)}>, <Entity(u'Drive',
5682617542246400L) {u'filekey':
'0d5b1/20171121233215/121659/image.jpg', u'empid': '121659',
u'timestamp': '20171121233215', u'created': datetime.datetime(2017,
11, 22, 4, 32, 16, 601877, tzinfo=<UTC>)}>]
========================
```

5. Now, let's use the Console to see all the files uploaded by employee ID `121659`.

6. Navigate to the **Cloud Datastore | Entities** page and click on **Query by GQL**.

7. The `select * from Drive where empid = '121659'` query should list down all the files uploaded by employee ID `121659`, as shown in the following screenshot:

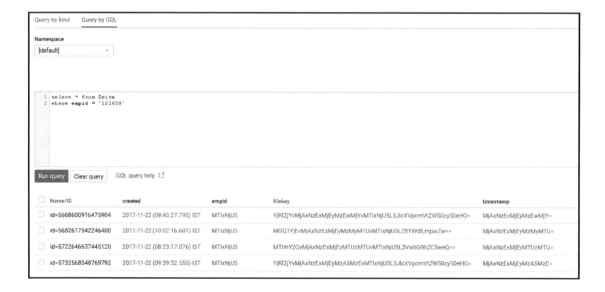

8. You can also write a simple Python script to query the files uploaded by an employee.

There's more...

We have written the `insert into the metadata` table along with the object upload in our Python code. However, this would rarely be an ideal scenario. The `upload` and the `insert into the metadata` table have to be decoupled. The elegant way to handle this is by using Cloud Functions. On the upload of the object, a Cloud Function can read the input file and update the metadata table. So, the update to the metadata table need not be close to the file upload and can be an independent function.

Networking 3

In this chapter, we will cover:

- Network management using a data network and a management network
- Content-based load balancing
- VPC network peering between two networks
- VPN connection between two networks
- CDN setup for a static website

Introduction

In this chapter, we'll discover some networking features of **Google Cloud Platform** (GCP). Google uses a state-of-the-art software-defined network to provide the networking feature for its customers. The networking unit of encapsulation for a set of IP ranges, firewall configurations,and VPN and routing configurations is the **Virtual Private Cloud** (VPC). VPCs can be scoped globally or regionally and are designed for high levels of security isolation and scalability. It is also possible to share the VPCs among projects.

In this chapter, we'll perform some recipes using multiple **network interface cards** (NICs), discover advanced features of load balancing and connect two VPCs using peering and a VPN connection.

In addition to its various VPC features, GCP also offers dedicated network services for DNS and CDN. We'll create a static website using Google Storage and put it behind Google CDN and measure its performance from varied locations.

Network management using a data and a management network

It is a common scenario in large servers to have more than one NIC for purposes demanded by the software to function properly, or for networking reasons. GCP allows a maximum of eight NICs (depending on the instance type) to be attached to an instance with `nic0` being the default NIC to which GCP's DHCP server sends a default route and `nic1` to `nic7` being optional.

In this recipe, we'll create an instance with two NICs with each of the NICs attached to a different network. One network would be a management network to manage the instance and another network, a data network, used to serve data to the public domain.

Getting ready

The following are the initial setup verifications and network creation to be carried out before the recipe can be executed:

1. Create or select a GCP project.
2. Enable billing and enable the default APIs (some APIs such as BigQuery, storage, monitoring, and a few others are enabled automatically).

3. We'll create the management network called `alpha-mgmt`. Choose, the **Custom** option for the **Subnet creation mode** and create a single subnet called `alpha-mgmt-us-central1` with an IP range of `10.2.0.0/24`. Leave the default value in the other fields:

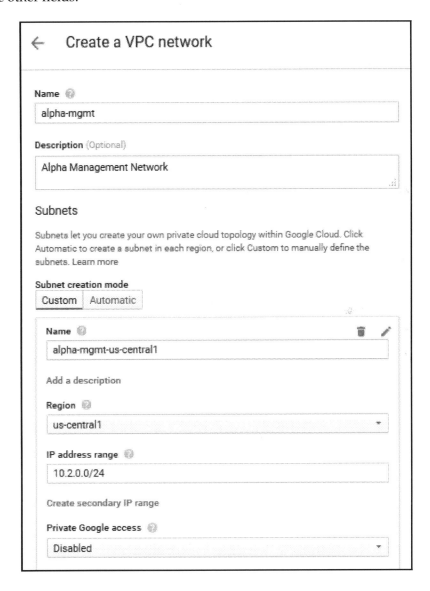

4. Next, we'll create our data network called `beta-data`. Choose the
   Automatic option under **Subnet creation mode**:

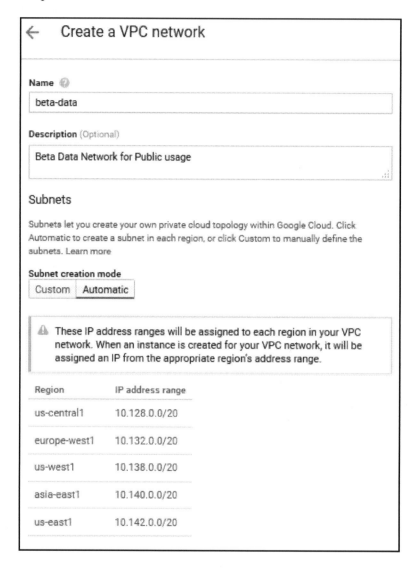

5. Let's not select any of the firewall rules for the moment. Click the **Create** button
   to provision the `beta-data` network.

How to do it...

We'll create a web server whose public web traffic (data) will be served by the `beta-data` network and the SSH into the web server would be via the `alpha-mgmt` network:

1. Firstly, we'll set up some firewall rules to the alpha and beta networks. In the `alpha-mgmt` network, open the SSH port `22` to all servers with the network tag `alpha-server`:

```
gcloud compute --project=<project id> firewall-rules create
allow-ssh-alpha-servers
--description="Allow ssh access to all servers with network tag
alpha-server"
--direction=INGRESS --priority=1000 --network=alpha-mgmt
--action=ALLOW --rules=tcp:22 --source-ranges=0.0.0.0/0
--target-tags=alpha-server
```

The created rule on the Console will be similar to the following screenshot:

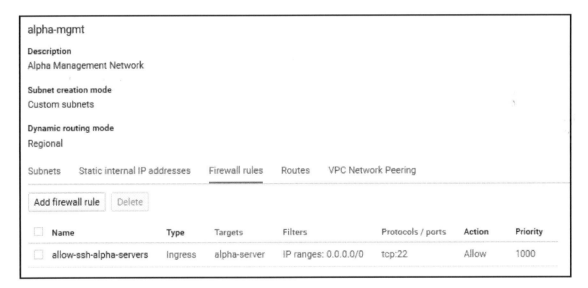

2. In the beta network, open access to the HTTP port 80 for all the servers tagged `beta-server` and `http-server`. This will allow the web traffic to flow to the web server:

```
gcloud compute --project=<project id> firewall-rules
create allow-http-beta-servers --description="allow http port 80"
--direction=INGRESS --priority=1000 --network=beta-data
--action=ALLOW --rules=tcp:80 --source-ranges=0.0.0.0/0
--target-tags=beta-server,http-server
```

The created firewall wall rule is shown in the following screenshot:

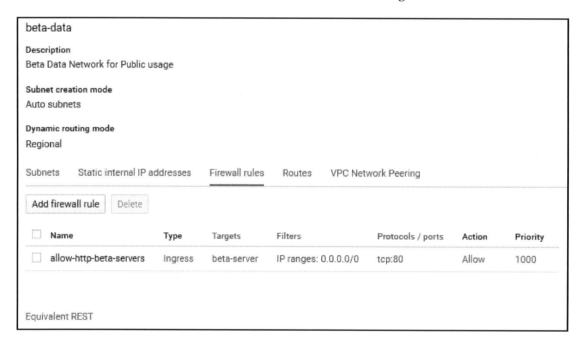

3. Next, we'll create our web instance which will have two NICs, one attached to the alpha network and the other to the beta network:

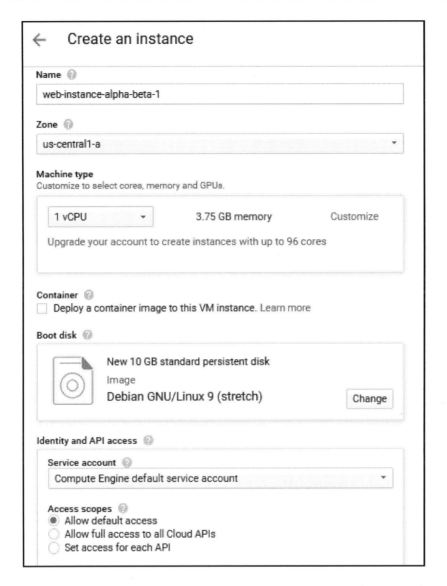

4. Next, click on the hyperlink **Management, disks, networking, SSH keys** to open the subtabs.

5. In the **Management** subtab, enter the following start up script:

```
#! /bin/bash
apt-get update
apt-get install -y apache2
cat <<EOF > /var/www/html/index.html
<html><body><h1>Hello World</h1>
<p>Web server on the alpha and beta networks</p>
</body></html>
EOF
```

The following screenshot shows the example for the preceding step:

6. Under the **Networking** subtab, add three network tabs, namely `alpha-server`, `beta-server`, and `http-server`.

7. Then, add two network interfaces, one under the `alpha-mgmt` network and the second one under the `beta-data` network. For now, let the instance have both internal and external IPs for both the networks:

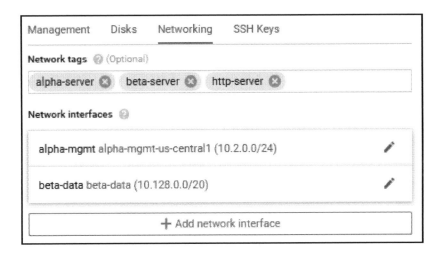

8. Click on the **Create** button to launch the instance creation.

9. The instance gets two public IPs, one for each NIC. However, the web page is not accessible because, in the alpha network, port `80` is not opened. And, in the beta network, though the port `80` is opened, the policy routing is not configured and so traffic does not flow through the second NIC.

10. Now, let's configure the policy routing for the `beta-data` network's NIC. From the **Compute Engine** home page, click on **SSH** against our instance:

```
$ sudo ifconfig eth1  10.128.0.2 netmask 255.255.255.255 broadcast
10.128.0.2 mtu 1430
$ sudo su -
$ sudo echo "1 rt1" >> /etc/iproute2/rt_tables
$ sudo ip route add  10.128.0.1 src  10.128.0.2 dev eth1
$ sudo ip route add default via  10.128.0.1 dev eth1 table rt1
$ sudo ip rule add from  10.128.0.2/32 table rt1
$ sudo ip rule add to  10.128.0.2/32 table rt1
```

11. Now that traffic can come in and exit via the beta-network NIC, launch your favorite browser and enter the public IP of the beta network of our instance. The web page loads:

12. We are done with the public network part, we'll now secure the management access to our web instance. We'll remove the public IP assignment for the `alpha-mgmt` network. Edit our web instance and under the network interfaces section, edit the `alpha-mgmt` NIC and select **None** for the **External IP**:

13. After the external IP has been removed, the web instance loses its default SSH capability from the web console.

14. To manage our web instance, let's create another instance in the `alpha-mgmt` network:

```
$ gcloud compute instances create "alpha-mgmt-instance-1" --project
"gcp-cookbook" --zone "us-central1-a" --machine-type "n1-
standard-1" --subnet "alpha-mgmt-us-central1" --image "debian-9-
stretch-v20171213" --image-project "debian-cloud" --boot-disk-size
"10"
--boot-disk-type "pd-standard" --boot-disk-device-name "alphamgmt-
instance-1" --scopes
"https://www.googleapis.com/auth/compute,https://www.googleapis.com
/auth/servicecontrol,https://www.googleapis.com/auth/service.manage
ment.readonly,https://www.googleapis.com/auth/logging.write,
https://www.googleapis.com/auth/monitoring.write,https://www.google
apis.com/auth/trace.append,https://www.googleapis.com/auth/devstora
ge.read_only"
```

15. From the VM console, click on the SSH for our new `alpha-mgmt-instance-1`. Most likely, you'll not have SSH access to the machine because the port 22 is open only to those instances network-tagged `alpha-server`. Let's edit the instance to add the network tag:

16. Now you'll be able to SSH into the `alpha-mgmt-instance-1`. From the alpha instance, we'll be able to SSH into our web instance as both of them are part of the alpha network. In the `alpha-mgmt-instance1`, use the following command to list all the instances and make sure the compute API is working properly:

```
user@alpha-mgmt-instance-1:~$ gcloud compute instances list
NAME ZONE MACHINE_TYPE PREEMPTIBLE INTERNAL_IP EXTERNAL_IP STATUS
alpha-mgmt-instance-1 us-central1-a n1-standard-1 10.2.0.3
35.193.87.74 RUNNING
web-instance-alpha-beta-1 us-central1-a n1-standard-1
10.2.0.2,10.128.0.2 35.226.255.176 RUNNING
```

17. Use the `beta compute` command and the option `--internal-ip` to SSH using the private IP address:

```
user@alpha-mgmt-instance-1:~$ gcloud beta compute ssh web-instance-
alpha-beta-1 --internal-ip
WARNING: The public SSH key file for gcloud does not exist.
WARNING: The private SSH key file for gcloud does not exist.
WARNING: You do not have an SSH key for gcloud.
WARNING: SSH keygen will be executed to generate a key.
Generating public/private rsa key pair.
Enter passphrase (empty for no passphrase):
Enter same passphrase again:
Your identification has been saved in
/home/<user>/.ssh/google_compute_engine.
Your public key has been saved in
/home/<user>/.ssh/google_compute_engine.pub.
The key fingerprint is:
SHA256:8FUmh9Ov17MzHV4BiBC+D9t8Dc1URYe9iqcpMv/hZ3o lego_aws@alpha-
mgmt-instance-1
The key's randomart image is:
+---[RSA 2048]----+
|      oo oo=  ==|
|       . .o*..o o|
|       ..  .. o. .|
|      o.. + .o |
+----[SHA256]-----+
Did you mean zone [us-central1-a] for instance:
[web-instance-alpha-beta-1] (Y/n)?  Y
Updating project ssh metadata...|Updated
[https://www.googleapis.com/compute/beta/projects/gcp-cookbook].
Updating project ssh metadata...done.
Waiting for SSH key to propagate.
Warning: Permanently added 'compute.5267467757986013353' (ECDSA) to
the list of known hosts.
  % Total    % Received % Xferd  Average Speed   Time    Time
```

```
Time   Current
                                  Dload  Upload   Total    Spent
Left   Speed
100    19 100    19    0     0   2348      0 --:--:-- --:--:-- --
:--:--  2375
Linux web-instance-alpha-beta-1 4.9.0-4-amd64 #1 SMP Debian
4.9.65-3 (2017-12-03) x86_64
The programs included with the Debian GNU/Linux system are free
software;
the exact distribution terms for each program are described in the
individual files in /usr/share/doc/*/copyright.
Debian GNU/Linux comes with ABSOLUTELY NO WARRANTY, to the extent
permitted by applicable law.
g284284611269_compute@web-instance-alpha-beta-1:~$
```

18. The web instance is connected to two networks—a management network for administration and a public-facing network for internet traffic.

There's more...

There are various scenarios which necessitate multiple NICs; a few configurations are discussed at `https://cloud.google.com/vpc/docs/multiple-interfaces-concepts`.

Content-based load balancing

GCP offers different kinds of load-balancing options for HTTP/HTTPS requests, SSL (TLS) connections, and non-HTTP TCP traffic. In addition, there are two other types of load balancing for advanced use cases; an internal load balancer for internal TCP/UDP-based traffic and a network load balancer for all other TCP/UDP and SSL traffic on ports that are not supported by the standard HTTP/HTTPS, SSL proxy, and TCP proxy load balancers.

In this recipe, we'll create a simple HTTP load balancer that will route traffic; based on the content requested.

Our HTTP load balancer will be configured such that:

- All URL paths starting with **/image** will be routed to the instance group **image** to serve the images for the website
- All URL paths starting with **/static** will be routed to our Google Storage bucket to serve static content

- All the other URL paths will be routed to the instance group **web**:

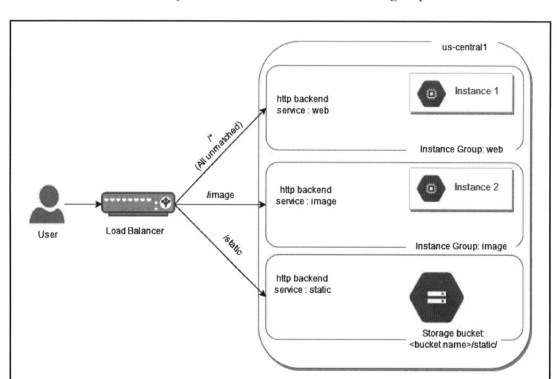

Getting ready

The following are the initial setup verifications to be carried out before the recipe can be executed:

1. Create or select a GCP project
2. Enable billing and enable the default APIs (some APIs such as BigQuery, storage, monitoring, and a few others are enabled automatically)
3. Install the `gcloud` and `gsutil` command-line tools

How to do it...

For this recipe, we'll follow these steps:

1. Create a web instance for normal traffic
2. Map the instance to the web instance group
3. Create another instance for image traffic
4. Map this instance to the video instance group
5. Create a firewall rule to allow `tcp:80` for all servers tagged `http-server`
6. Create a bucket and a static folder for static content
7. Create a health check that will be used for the load balancer configuration
8. Create a load balancer with content-based routing rules for web, image, and static content

We'll see the preceding steps in details as follows:

1. Create the web instance and install Apache using the start up script. We'll also add the network tag `http-server` to be used by our firewall rules:

```
gcloud compute instances create web-server \
--image-family debian-9 \
--image-project debian-cloud \
--zone us-central1-b \
--tags http-server \
--metadata startup-script="#! /bin/bash
   sudo apt-get update
   sudo apt-get install apache2 -y
   sudo service apache2 restart
   echo '<!doctype html><html><body><h1>Web Server</h1></body>
   </html>' | sudo tee /var/www/html/index.html
   EOF"
```

2. Create an unmanaged instance group and add our web server to the web group:

```
gcloud compute instance-groups unmanaged create web-group \
--zone us-central1-b

gcloud compute instance-groups unmanaged add-instances web-group \
--instances web-server \
--zone us-central1-b
```

3. We'll repeat the same two steps for our `image-server` too. Note that we are creating an `image` folder under Apache's root folder so that the load balancer will serve traffic from the `/image` directory:

```
gcloud compute instances create image-server \
--image-family debian-9 \
--image-project debian-cloud \
--zone us-central1-b \
--tags http-server \
--metadata startup-script="#! /bin/bash
  sudo apt-get update
  sudo apt-get install apache2 -y
  sudo service apache2 restart
  echo '<!doctype html><html><body><h1>Image Server</h1>
  </body></html>' | sudo tee /var/www/html/index.html
  sudo mkdir /var/www/html/image
  echo '<!doctype html><html><body><h1>Image Server</h1>
  </body></html>' | sudo tee /var/www/html/image/index.html
  EOF"

gcloud compute instance-groups unmanaged create image-group \
--zone us-central1-b

gcloud compute instance-groups unmanaged add-instances image-group \
--instances image-server \
--zone us-central1-b
```

4. Once the two instances and two instance groups are created, you can view the resources using the `gcloud` command or on the Console:

	Name ^	Zone	Recommendation	Internal IP	External IP	Connect	
☐ ⊘	image-server	us-central1-b		10.128.0.2	35.188.75.19 ⤤	SSH ▾	⋮
☐ ⊘	web-server	us-central1-b		10.128.0.4	104.198.79.167 ⤤	SSH ▾	⋮

5. In the following screenshot, you can view the details of the two instance groups that were created:

	Name ∧	Zone	Creation time	Instances	Template	Recommendation	Autoscaling	In use by
	image-group	us-central1-b	Dec 29, 2017, 11:24:34 AM	1	--			
	web-group	us-central1-b	Dec 29, 2017, 11:19:04 AM	1	--			

6. Both the servers created are not accessible from the internet. Let's open the firewall for HTTP traffic on these two instances:

```
gcloud compute firewall-rules create http-firewall --target-tags
http-server --allow tcp:80
```

7. Now, the external IPs on the two instances are accessible:

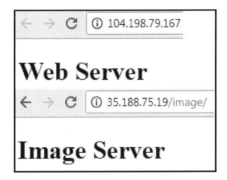

8. We'll also create a health check that will be later used in our load balancer configuration:

```
gcloud compute health-checks create http http-health-check
```

The following screenshot shows the output for the preceding command:

	Name ∧	Host	Path	Protocol	Port	In use by
	http-health-check		/	HTTP	80	

9. Next, for our static content, let's create a new bucket:

```
gsutil mb gs://gcp-bk-content-filtering/
```

10. We can upload any static content to be used by our web page to this bucket, for example an image, CSS files or JS files. For simplicity, we'll upload a thumbnail image to the bucket to be used by our load balancer. Make sure that the object is uploaded under the `static` path, as this will be later used in our load balancer configuration:

```
gsutil cp GCP1.png gs://gcp-bk-content-filtering/static/GCP1.png
```

The following screenshot shows the output for the preceding command:

11. We should also make the object publicly readable so that everyone can read the object via the load balancer:

```
gsutil acl ch -u AllUsers:R gs://gcp-bk-content-
filtering/static/GCP1.png
```

12. Now that all the resource providers are created, we'll get into the meat of this recipe to configure the load-balancer. Go to the load balancing page of the Console and click on **Create load balancer**.

13. Then click on **Start Configuration** under the **HTTP(S) Load Balancing** tile. Give a name to the load balancer and click on **Backend configuration**:

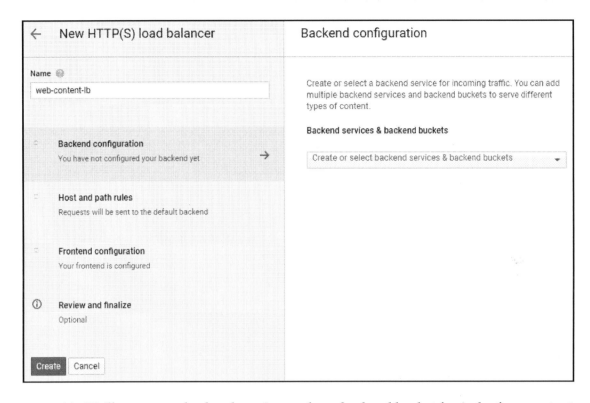

14. We'll create two backend services and one backend bucket for each of our content types:
    1. Click on **Create a backend service** from the drop-down menu:

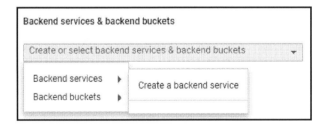

    2. Fill in the details for the new backend service to serve traffic from our web server:
        - **Name**: Give the name `web-backend-service`.
        - **Backends**: Select `web-group` from the drop-down menu. Leave the default port number as `80`.

- **Health check**: Select `http-health-check` from the drop-down menu. Leave the defaults in the rest of the fields and click **Create**:

3. Similarly, create another backend service for the image traffic from our `image-server`:

   - **Name**: Give the name `image-backend-service`.
   - **Backends**: Select `web-group` from the drop-down menu. Leave the default port number as `80`.
   - **Health check**: Select `http-health-check` from the drop-down menu. Leave the defaults in the rest of the fields and click **Create**.

15. Select **Create a backend bucket** from the drop-down menu. Give the name `static-thumbnail-bucket` and select the storage bucket created by clicking the **Browse** button. Then click **Create**:

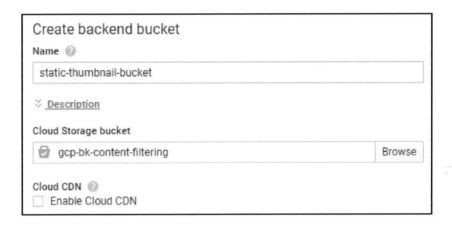

16. Now the **Backend configuration** is complete:

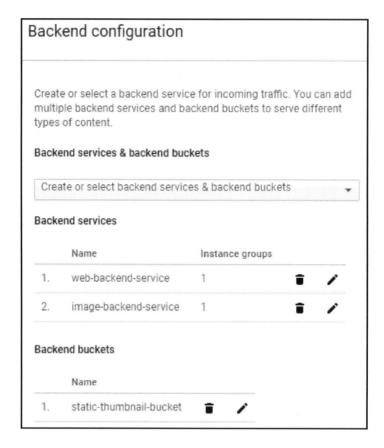

17. Next, let's configure the **Host and path rules**:
    - The first row is autopopulated with the default rule directing traffic to `web-backend-service`.
    - For the second row, set **Hosts** to `*` and **Paths** to `/image` and `/image/*`.
    - For the third row, set **Hosts** to `*` and **Paths** to `/static/*`:

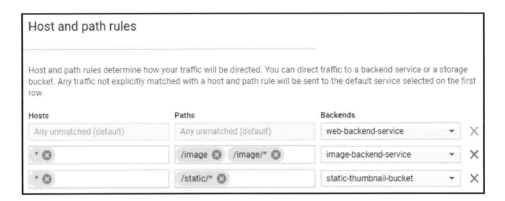

18. Next, from the left panel, click on **Frontend configuration**. Set up a rule for HTTP traffic on port 80. Give the name `http-web-rule`, leave the rest as defaults and click on the **Done** button:

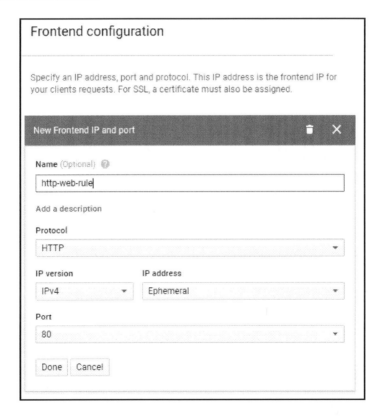

19. To review, on the left panel click on **Review and finalize**. Verify if everything looks OK and then click **Create** to create the HTTP(S) load balancer.

20. To verify that the load balancer is serving traffic as intended, confirm that the instances are healthy by verifying the **Healthy** column of our backend services:

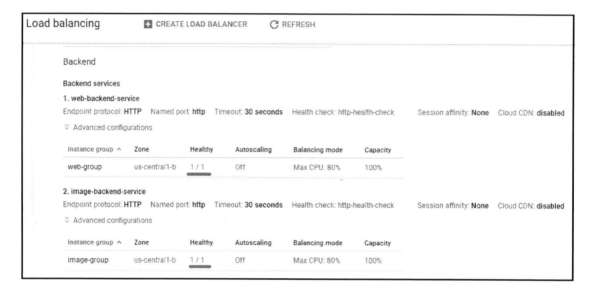

21. Now, we can point to our different URLs to confirm that the load balancer is directing traffic to our different resources. The IP address of the load balancer can be found under the **Frontends** tab:

    1. On the browser, point to the address of the load balancer:

    2. Using the `/image` URL, our load balancer hits the `image-server`:

3. And for the static thumbnail to be served from the storage bucket, point the URL to `/static/<object name>`:

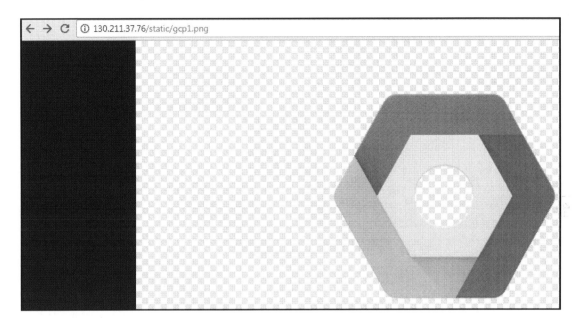

22. Now, we have tested our load balancer to perform content-based routing.

 If you face any access issues when accessing the thumbnail image from the storage bucket, verify the permissions on the object accessed. To make an existing object publicly readable from a bucket, you can use: **gsutil acl ch −u AllUsers:R gs://<bucket name>/****.

VPC network peering between two networks

VPC is GCP's network encapsulation with its own address space and set of resources. For instances from one VPC to communicate with an instance in another VPC, they can route traffic via the open internet. However, to communicate between privately two VPCs, GCP offers a service called VPC peering. We can create a peering connection without any project or organizational restrictions. VPC peering reduces network latency, improves security and network costs by communicating via internal IPs.

For more information refer to: `https://cloud.google.com/vpc/docs/vpc-peering`.

Getting ready

The following are the initial setup verification steps and network creation to be carried out before the recipe can be executed:

1. Create or select a GCP project.
2. Enable billing and enable the default APIs (some APIs such as BigQuery, storage, monitoring, and a few others are enabled automatically).
3. We'll create a VPC network called `alpha`. The following command assumes that you have set your default project:

   ```
   gcloud compute networks create alpha --subnet-mode=custom
   ```

4. Next, let's create a single subnet called `alpha-subnet-1` with an IP range of `192.168.0.0/16`:

   ```
   gcloud compute networks subnets create alpha-subnet-1
   --network=alpha --region=us-central1 --range=192.168.0.0/16
   ```

5. Similarly, let's create a beta VPC network with a single subnet with a different IP range `10.1.0.0/24`:

   ```
   gcloud compute networks create beta --subnet-mode=custom
   ```

   ```
   gcloud compute networks subnets create beta-subnet-1 --network=beta
   --region=us-central1 --range=10.1.0.0/24
   ```

6. The network setup will look similar to the following screenshot:

Name ^	Region	Subnets	Mode	IP addresses ranges	Gateways	Firewall Rules	Global dynamic routing
alpha		1	Custom			0	Off
	us-central1	alpha-subnet-1		192.168.0.0/16	192.168.0.1		
beta		1	Custom			0	Off
	us-central1	beta-subnet-1		10.1.0.0/24	10.1.0.1		

VPC networks   CREATE VPC NETWORK   REFRESH

How to do it...

Once the network and subnets are created, we'll create instances in the subnets and try to establish a communication. As there is no connectivity, the communication will fail. Next, we'll establish VPC peering to connect the two networks and verify the communication between the instance created:

1. Let's create a VM in the subnet `alpha-subnet-1` with default attributes:

```
gcloud beta compute instances create "alpha-instance" \
--zone "us-central1-a" --machine-type "n1-standard-1" \
--subnet "alpha-subnet-1" --image "debian-9-stretch-v20171213" \
--image-project "debian-cloud"
```

2. We'll create a firewall rule for all SSH and ICMP traffic in the network `alpha`:

```
gcloud compute firewall-rules create alpha-firewall --network alpha
--allow tcp:22,icmp --source-ranges 0.0.0.0/0
```

3. Similarly, let's create another VM in the `beta-subnet-1` and the firewall rule for the `beta` network:

```
gcloud beta compute instances create "beta-instance" \
--zone "us-central1-a" --machine-type "n1-standard-1" \
--subnet "beta-subnet-1" --image "debian-9-stretch-v20171213" \
--image-project "debian-cloud"

gcloud compute firewall-rules create beta-firewall --network beta
--allow tcp:22,icmp --source-ranges 0.0.0.0/0
```

4. After the VMs are created, their public and private IPs are populated:

	Name ^	Zone	Recommendation	Internal IP	External IP	Connect	
☐ ✅	alpha-instance	us-central1-a		192.168.0.2	104.198.73.228	SSH ▾	⋮
☐ ✅	beta-instance	us-central1-a		10.1.0.2	35.226.118.252	SSH ▾	⋮

5. From the Console, SSH into the VMs in the `alpha` network. From the Console, determine the internal IP address of the beta VM and try to ping it from the alpha VM:

```
$ ping 10.1.0.2PING 10.1.0.2 (10.1.0.2) 56(84) bytes of data.
^C
--- 10.1.0.2 ping statistics ---
3 packets transmitted, 0 received, 100% packet loss, time 2031ms
```

6. You'll notice that the VM on the `beta` network is not reachable from the `alpha` network. Perform a similar test from the machine on the `beta` network to the machine on the `alpha` network.

7. Now, to enable connectivity between the two VPCs, let's create a VPC peering connection.

8. From the **VPC Network Peering** submenu, click on **Create connection**. After reading the requirements, click on **Continue**.

9. Create the first leg of the peering connection from the `alpha` network to the `beta` network as follows:

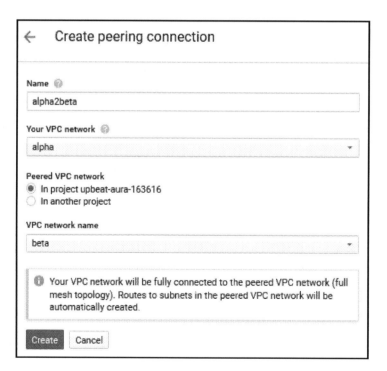

10. Next, the second leg is as follows:

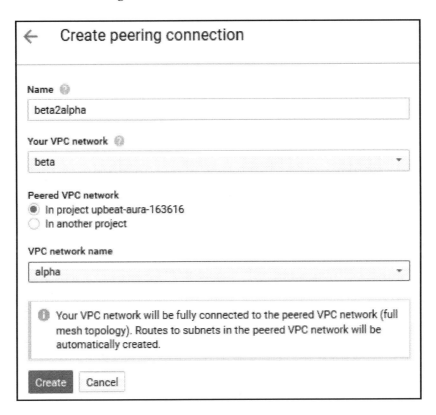

11. After both the peering connections are created, the **Status** of the connections shows **Connected**:

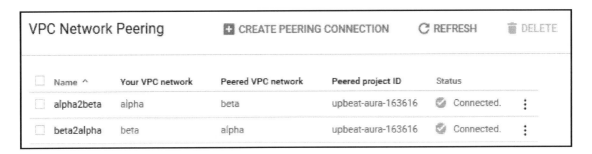

12. Perform the connectivity test from the VM from the `alpha` network to the VM on the `beta` network, as in *step 5*:

```
========== alpha-instance to beta-instance ==================
$ ping 10.1.0.2
PING 10.1.0.2 (10.1.0.2) 56(84) bytes of data.
64 bytes from 10.1.0.2: icmp_seq=1 ttl=64 time=0.156 ms
64 bytes from 10.1.0.2: icmp_seq=2 ttl=64 time=0.228 ms
64 bytes from 10.1.0.2: icmp_seq=3 ttl=64 time=0.193 ms
^C
--- 10.1.0.2 ping statistics ---
3 packets transmitted, 3 received, 0% packet loss, time 2041msrtt
min/avg/max/mdev = 0.156/0.192/0.228/0.031 ms

========== beta-instance to alpha-instance ==================
$ ping 192.168.0.2
PING 192.168.0.2 (192.168.0.2) 56(84) bytes of data.
64 bytes from 192.168.0.2: icmp_seq=1 ttl=64 time=0.885 ms
|64 bytes from 192.168.0.2: icmp_seq=2 ttl=64 time=0.189 ms
64 bytes from 192.168.0.2: icmp_seq=3 ttl=64 time=0.168 ms
^C
--- 192.168.0.2 ping statistics ---
3 packets transmitted, 3 received, 0% packet loss, time 2033msrtt
min/avg/max/mdev = 0.168/0.414/0.885/0.333 ms
```

13. Now, with VPC peering, the VMs on the two VPCs (alpha and beta) are able to communicate via their internal IPs.

VPN connection between two networks

Similar to the previous recipe, another way to establish a connection between two networks is via a VPN connection. Usually, a VPN connection is used to connect an on-premises network with GCP via an IPSEC tunnel. However, for all learning purposes, connecting two VPCs gives us a good understanding of how to go about a VPN setup.

Getting ready

The following are the initial setup verification steps and network creation to be carried out before the recipe can be executed:

1. Create or select a GCP project.
2. Enable billing and enable the default APIs (some APIs such as BigQuery, storage, monitoring, and a few others are enabled automatically).
3. Similar to the previous recipe, we'll create a VPC network called `alpha-nw`. The following command assumes that you have set your default project:

   ```
   gcloud compute networks create alpha-nw --subnet-mode=custom
   ```

4. Next, let's create a single subnet called `alpha-subnet-1` with an IP range of `192.168.0.0/16`:

   ```
   gcloud compute networks subnets create alpha-subnet-vpn \
   --network=alpha-nw --region=us-east1 --range=10.1.0.0/16
   ```

5. Similarly, let's create a beta VPC network with a single subnet with a different IP range `10.2.0.0/24`:

   ```
   gcloud compute networks create beta-nw --subnet-mode=custom

   gcloud compute networks subnets create beta-subnet-vpn \
   --network=beta-nw --region=us-central1 --range=10.2.0.0/24
   ```

6. Let's also create the firewall rules to allow SSH and ICMP on the two networks created:

   ```
   gcloud compute firewall-rules create alpha-nw-firewall --network
   alpha-nw --allow tcp:22,icmp --source-ranges 0.0.0.0/0

   gcloud compute firewall-rules create beta-nw-firewall --network
   beta-nw --allow tcp:22,icmp --source-ranges 0.0.0.0/0
   ```

7. The two networks and their subnet will look similar to the following screenshot:

Name ∧	Region	Subnets	Mode	IP addresses ranges	Gateways	Firewall Rules	Global dynamic routing
alpha-nw		1	Custom			1	Off
	us-east1	alpha-subnet-vpn		10.1.0.0/16	10.1.0.1		
beta-nw		1	Custom			1	Off
	us-central1	beta-subnet-vpn		10.2.0.0/24	10.2.0.1		

VPC networks — CREATE VPC NETWORK — REFRESH

8. Let's create two static IPs in the two regions (`us-east1` and `us-central1`) where our subnets are created. These static IPs will be used during our VPN setup:

   ```
   gcloud compute addresses create alpha-static-ip --region=us-east1
   ```

   ```
   gcloud compute addresses create beta-static-ip --region=us-central1
   ```

9. Now, the static IPs look like the following in the Console (**VPN Network | External IP addresses**):

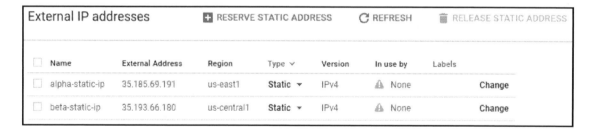

External IP addresses — RESERVE STATIC ADDRESS — REFRESH — RELEASE STATIC ADDRESS

Name	External Address	Region	Type ∨	Version	In use by	Labels	
alpha-static-ip	35.185.69.191	us-east1	Static ▾	IPv4	⚠ None		Change
beta-static-ip	35.193.66.180	us-central1	Static ▾	IPv4	⚠ None		Change

How to do it...

Initially, the instances in the subnets created will not have connectivity. We'll setup a VPN connection and verify that we are able to establish a connection between the instances in the two separate networks:

1. Let's create a VM in the subnet `alpha-subnet-vpn` with default attributes:

   ```
   gcloud beta compute instances create "alpha-instance" --zone
   "us-east1-c" --machine-type "n1-standard-1" --subnet
   "alpha-subnet-vpn" --image "debian-9-stretch-v20171213"
   --image-project "debian-cloud"
   ```

2. Similarly, let's create another VM in the `beta-subnet-vpn`:

   ```
   gcloud beta compute instances create "beta-instance" --zone
   "us-central1-c" --machine-type "n1-standard-1" --subnet
   "beta-subnet-vpn" --image "debian-9-stretch-v20171213"
   --image-project "debian-cloud"
   ```

3. After the VMs are created, their public and private IPs are populated:

4. From the Console, SSH into the VMs in the `alpha` network. From the Console, determine the internal IP address of the `beta-instance` VM and try to ping it from the alpha VM:

   ```
   $ ping 10.2.0.2PING 10.1.0.2 (10.1.0.2) 56(84) bytes of data.
   ^C
   --- 10.2.0.2 ping statistics ---
   3 packets transmitted, 0 received, 100% packet loss, time 2053ms
   ```

5. You'll notice that the VM on the beta network is not reachable from the `alpha` network. Perform a similar test from the machine on the beta network to the machine on the `alpha` network.

6. To connect the two networks, we'll need a VPN connection. First, let's create the VPN connection on the `alpha` network. On the Google Console, navigate to **Hybrid Connectivity** | **VPN** and click on **Create VPN connection**:

   1. Give the name `alpha-vpn`.

   2. From the **Network** drop-down menu, select the `alpha-nw`.

   3. Select the `us-east1` region.

   4. From the **IP address** drop-down menu, select the static address `alpha-static-ip` that we have already created:

7. In the second part of the setup, we'll provide the tunnel details:

1. For the **Remote peer IP address**, get the static IP reserved (`beta-static-ip`) on the `us-central1` and insert it here.

2. Provide a secret text in the **Shared secret**, we'll have to provide the same secret text for the VPN created on the beta network.

3. In the **Routing options** field, choose the **Static** option. Provide the IP address range of the `beta-subnet-vpn` (`10.2.0.0/24`) here.

4. Finally, in the **Local subnetworks**, select our `alpha-subnet-vpn`.

5. Click on **Create** to create the VPN connection:

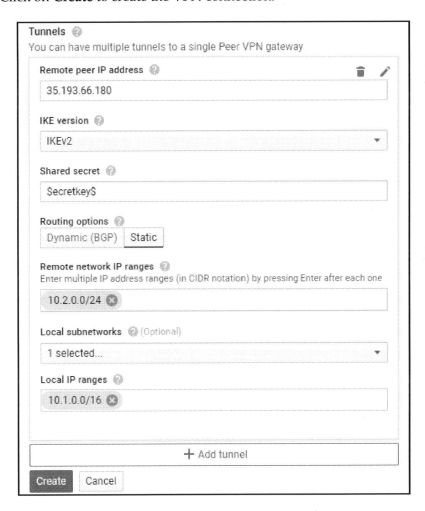

8. In the same fashion, let's create a VPN connection on the beta network:

9. Fill in the required information as shown:

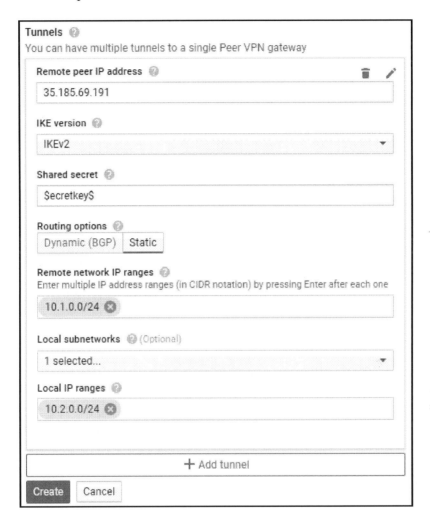

10. Once both the VPN connections are created, the VPN tunnels come into service:

Name	Network	Region	IP address	Remote peer IP address		Cloud routers	Logs	Firewall rules
VPN **CREATE VPN CONNECTION** **REFRESH** DELETE								
alpha-vpn	alpha-nw	us-east1	35.185.69.191	✔ 35.193.66.180		None	View	Configure
beta-vpn	beta-nw	us-central1	35.193.66.180	✔ 35.185.69.191		None	View	Configure

11. Perform the same connectivity test from the instance on network alpha and the instance on network beta:

```
========== alpha-instance to beta-instance ==================
$ ping 10.2.0.2
PING 10.2.0.2 (10.2.0.2) 56(84) bytes of data.
64 bytes from 10.2.0.2: icmp_seq=1 ttl=64 time=39.6 ms
64 bytes from 10.2.0.2: icmp_seq=2 ttl=64 time=37.2 ms
64 bytes from 10.2.0.2: icmp_seq=3 ttl=64 time=36.9 ms
64 bytes from 10.2.0.2: icmp_seq=4 ttl=64 time=36.8 ms
^C
--- 10.2.0.2 ping statistics ---
4 packets transmitted, 4 received, 0% packet loss, time 3004ms
rtt min/avg/max/mdev = 36.897/37.674/39.639/1.157 ms

========== beta-instance to alpha-instance ==================
$ ping 10.1.0.2
PING 10.1.0.2 (10.1.0.2) 56(84) bytes of data.
64 bytes from 10.1.0.2: icmp_seq=1 ttl=64 time=39.1 ms
64 bytes from 10.1.0.2: icmp_seq=2 ttl=64 time=36.9 ms
64 bytes from 10.1.0.2: icmp_seq=3 ttl=64 time=36.9 ms
^C
--- 10.1.0.2 ping statistics ---
3 packets transmitted, 3 received, 0% packet loss, time 2002ms
rtt min/avg/max/mdev = 36.960/37.700/39.172/1.052 ms
```

12. With the VPN connection established between the alpha and beta networks, the ping test is successful from both the instances. The packet transfer data is captured in the VPN logs, and an example is shown as follows:

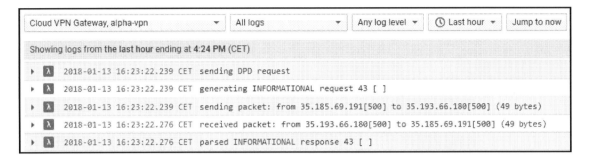

CDN setup for a static website

We hosted a static website on Google Storage in the previous chapter. In this recipe, we'll set up a Cloud CDN for another simple static site. Google Cloud CDN caches the contents of our static website in the globally distributed edge POPs. This helps bring the content faster to the end user and a reduction of the cost to serve from the data center.

We'll create a simple `index.html` and host it in our storage bucket. By putting this bucket behind a load balancer, we'll get an IP to hit our `index.html` file directly . As a second step, we'll set up a CDN and measure the increase in performance and explore the cache invalidation feature.

Getting ready

The following are the initial setup verification steps and static site creation to be carried out before the recipe can be executed:

1. Create or select a GCP project.
2. Enable billing and enable the default APIs (some APIs such as BigQuery, storage, monitoring, and a few others are enabled automatically).

3. Create a bucket with a unique name in a single region:

4. Create a simple `index.html` file and upload it to the bucket created:

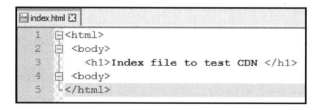

5. After uploading, here is what it will look like:

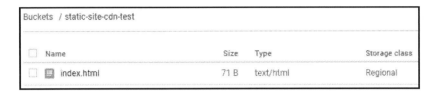

6. Check the box **Public link** to share the file to everyone. Click on the **Public link** to verify that the file is hosted properly:

How to do it...

With the `index.html` file hosted, we'll create a load balancer to frontend our bucket and put in behind the Cloud CDN:

1. In the Console, navigate to the **Network services** section and select **Load balancing**.
2. For our static site, we'll need an HTTP(S) load balancing. Click on **Start configuration** to start the setup.
3. Give a name to the load balancer and head to the **Backend configuration**:

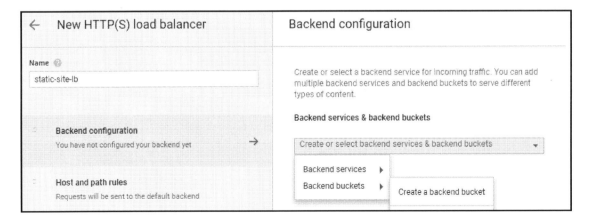

4. Create a backend bucket for our storage bucket:

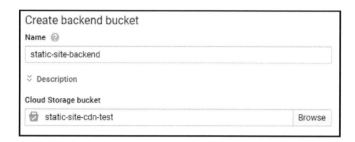

5. Once the backend bucket is created, click on the **Create** button to complete the load balancer's setup:

6. After a few minutes, we can use the frontend IP to view our `index.html` file from the browser:

7. With the bucket hosted in `us-central1`, let's measure the latency of our static website using `https://www.dotcom-tools.com`:

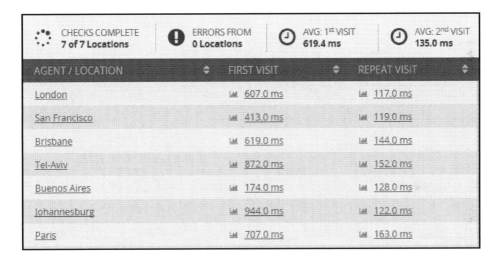

8. Next, let's put the static website behind the Cloud CDN. In the Console, select the **Cloud CDN** submenu and click on the **Add origin** button. From the drop-down menu, select the load balancer, `static-site-lb`, that we created in the previous steps and click on the **Add** button:

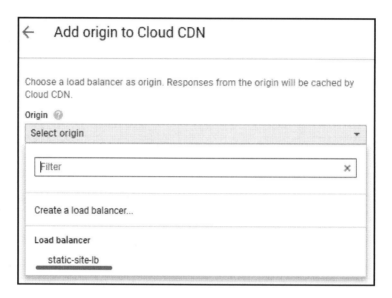

9. After the CDN is created for our static website, wait for a couple of minutes before the site is cached to the edge locations. If you run the latency test again, you'll see much-improved results as the contents are delivered from the nearest location:

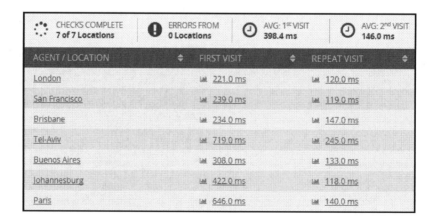

10. Head to the monitoring tab of the **Origin details**; you'll get what percentage of the requests and to which region the contents are delivered from the cache:

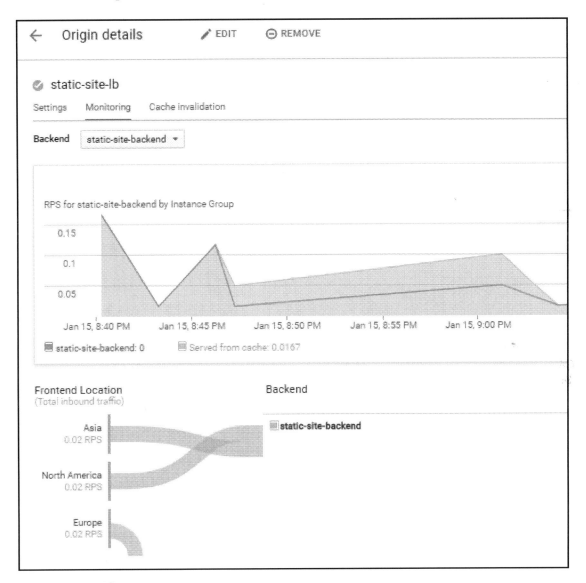

11. To understand the cache invalidation feature, let's update the `index.html` file and upload it. Navigate to the same frontend URL and observe the changes:

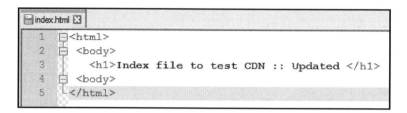

```
1  <html>
2    <body>
3      <h1>Index file to test CDN :: Updated </h1>
4    <body>
5  </html>
```

The cache invalidation feature:

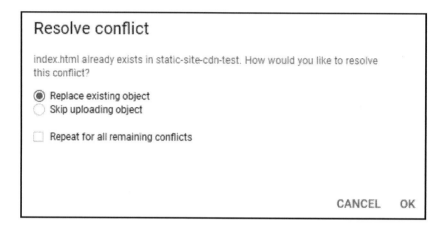

Resolve conflict

index.html already exists in static-site-cdn-test. How would you like to resolve this conflict?

⦿ Replace existing object
◯ Skip uploading object

☐ Repeat for all remaining conflicts

CANCEL   OK

12. Make sure you share the uploaded file publicly. In some locations, the change would be propagated and in some locations, the old data is seen, as shown here:

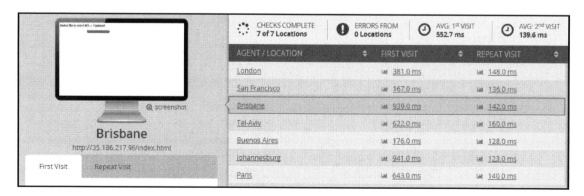

CHECKS COMPLETE 7 of 7 Locations	ERRORS FROM 0 Locations	AVG: 1st VISIT 552.7 ms	AVG: 2nd VISIT 139.6 ms
AGENT / LOCATION	**FIRST VISIT**	**REPEAT VISIT**	
London	381.0 ms	148.0 ms	
San Francisco	167.0 ms	136.0 ms	
Brisbane	939.0 ms	142.0 ms	
Tel-Aviv	622.0 ms	160.0 ms	
Buenos Aires	176.0 ms	128.0 ms	
Johannesburg	941.0 ms	123.0 ms	
Paris	643.0 ms	140.0 ms	

Brisbane
http://35.186.217.96/index.html

First Visit   Repeat Visit

The output in another location:

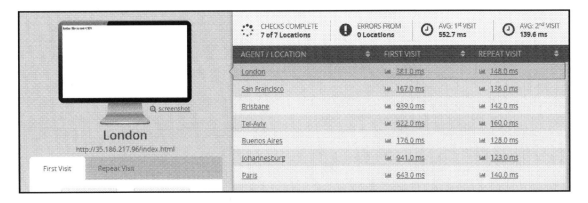

13. To make sure all the regions have the updated `index.html` data, we'll invalidate the cache in all the edge locations using the path of the file:

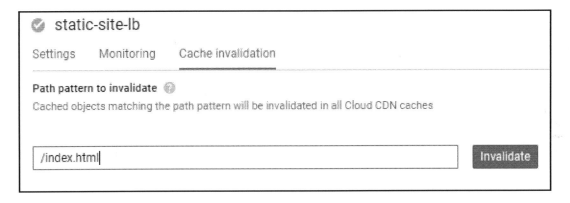

14. Once the cache invalidation operation is successful, all the regions will have the most recent data for `index.html`.

4
Security

In this chapter, we will cover the following topics:

- Scanning for vulnerabilities using Cloud Security Scanner
- Using Identity-Aware Proxy on App Engine
- Securing financial data using Cloud KMS
- Using the Data Loss Prevention API
- Creating IAM custom roles
- Creating service accounts
- Automatic recon and defense

Introduction

Security was, is, and always will be a critical point of discussion for any solution architecture. Google Cloud offers a range of services, catering to the information security needs of our solutions. Cloud IAM is an enterprise-grade IAM system, which securely enables admins to enable or deny access to **Google Cloud Platform (GCP)** services. Users of GCP can gain access at an organizational level, a group level, a project level, or at a resource level. We'll create a custom role to gain a better understanding of roles and of IAM in general. GCP offers a host of security services, such as Cloud **Identity-Aware Proxy (IAP)**, Cloud **Data Loss Prevention (DLP)**, Security Key Enforcement, Cloud **Key Management Service (KMS)**, Cloud Resource Manager and Cloud Security Scanner. We'll test a few of the services in this chapter.

 Read more about Google Cloud's security model here: `https://cloud.google.com/security/`.

Scanning for vulnerabilities using Cloud Security Scanner

Cloud Security Scanner is a service with App Engine that scans the web applications for security vulnerabilities. It detects cross-site scripting, flash injection, mixed content, and usage of unsecured JS libraries, by crawling through the starting URL of the App Engine. In this chapter, we'll see how to set up a security scan for a sample vulnerable application and review its results. After the scan is created, it is queued for execution. Depending on the size of the application, the time required for the scan ranges from a few minutes to a few hours.

Getting ready

The following are the initial setup verification steps, which are required before the recipe can be executed:

1. Create or select a GCP project
2. Enable billing and enable the default APIs (some APIs like BigQuery, storage, monitoring, and a few others are enabled automatically)
3. The owner, and editor of the project have full access to Cloud Security Scanner by default

How to do it...

We'll use a vulnerable app written in Python from `https://github.com/mpirnat/lets-be-bad-guys` and host it in our flexible App Engine environment. This site is developed for learning the most popular kinds of attacks on websites:

1. We'll use the Cloud Shell to deploy the application to App Engine. Launch the Cloud Shell, using the Activate Google Cloud Shell button or the following URL: `https://console.cloud.google.com/cloudshell`.
2. Clone the repository and navigate to the `lets-be-bad-guys` folder under `Chapter03`:

   ```
   $ git clone https://github.com/legorie/gcpcookbook.git
   cd gcpcookbook/Chapter03/lets-be-bad-guys
   ```

3. Have a look at the `app.yaml` file, which contains the configuration information for the deployment to the flexible environment:

```
[icons] Cloud Shell ×    +

@cloudshell:~/gcpcookbook/Chapter03/lets-be-bad-guys$ ls
app.yaml  badguys  LICENSE.txt  manage.py  README.md  requirements.txt  solutions.md
@cloudshell:~/gcpcookbook/Chapter03/lets-be-bad-guys$ cat app.yaml
# [START runtime]
runtime: python
env: flex
entrypoint: gunicorn -b :$PORT badguys.wsgi

runtime_config:
  python_version: 3.4
# [END runtime]
@cloudshell:~/gcpcookbook/Chapter03/lets-be-bad-guys$
```

Once, we have a code, create an isolated environment and install the dependencies:

```
virtualenv env
source env/bin/activate
pip install -r requirements.txt
```

4. After the dependencies are successfully installed, we can launch the Django local web server using the standard following command and verify the web application in the browser:

```
python manage.py runserver
```

The output of the preceding command can be seen in the following screenshot:

```
Performing system checks...

System check identified no issues (0 silenced).
January 20, 2018 - 14:46:01
Django version 1.9.6, using settings 'badguys.settings'
Starting development server at http://127.0.0.1:8000/
Quit the server with CONTROL-C.
```

5. Click on the development server URL to view the web application:

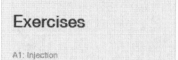

https://8000-dot-2960840-dot-devshell.appspot.com/?authuser=0

Shiny, Let's Be Bad Guys!
Exploiting and Mitigating the Top 10 Web App Vulnerabilities

| Exercises | Welcome to the Jungle |
| A1: Injection | |

6. Deploy the application to the App Engine flexible environment:

   ```
   gcloud app deploy --project=<Project Name>
   ```

7. Once the application is successfully deployed, navigate to the URL of the App Engine to view the application:

   ```
   gcloud app browse --project=<Project Name>
   ```

8. Next, we'll move on to the security scanning of the application. Navigate to the **Security scans** submenu under the **App Engine**.
9. Click on **Create scan** and, then, verify if the URL of the App Engine is autopopulated in the **STARTING URLS** textbox.
10. With all the default values, proceed to create the new scan.
11. Once the scan is created, click on the **RUN** button to start the scanning job.
12. After the completion of the scan, the results are reported:

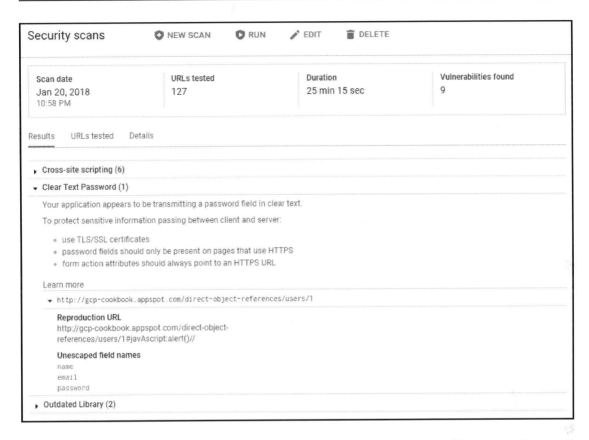

13. The scan reported nine vulnerabilities, as shown in the preceding screenshot, classified under three different headers.

How it works...

There is no special pricing to use the Cloud Security Scanner. The Scanner crawls through all the possible URLs exposed by the application and tests all the possible user inputs and event handlers. The Scanner targets the most crucial security risks listed on the OWASP Top Ten Project.

The Security Scanner is a strong ally to existing security testing, but it is never a replacement for a manual security review: `https://cloud.google.com/security-scanner/`.

Using Identity-Aware Proxy on App Engine

Cloud IAP verifies the identity of the person and controls access to our cloud applications hosted on GCP. Cloud IAP can be used with the App Engine and the Compute Engine. In our recipe, we'll use the application hosted on App Engine in our previous recipe and enable Cloud IAP. We'll see how, without any login page for the user, we are able to provide access to the application.

Getting ready

The following are the initial setup verification steps, which are required before the recipe can be executed:

1. Create or select a GCP project
2. Enable billing and enable the default APIs (some APIs like BigQuery, storage, monitoring, and a few others are enabled automatically)

How to do it...

With the `lets-be-bad-guys` application installed in our App Engine flexible environment, we will enable the IAP for this application:

1. Navigate to the **IAM & Admin** section and to the submenu **Identity-Aware Proxy**. You'll be able to see our App Engine application listed:

2. Configure the **OAuth consent screen**, as it is a prerequisite for enabling IAP:

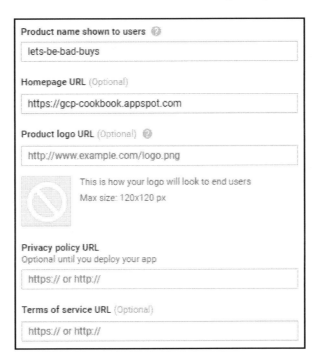

3. After setting up the OAuth screen, you'll be able to turn on the IAP option for our App Engine application. For this recipe, we are not using any custom domain, accept the default domain name provided and click on **TURN ON**:

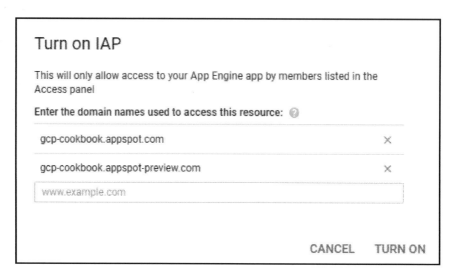

4. Once IAP is enabled, you'll see the configuration requirement flag is set to **OK**:

5. Now, if you navigate to our App Engine URL, you'll be prompted to login to an account. Try to log in using any available Gmail or G Suite account, you'll see a no-access page:

You don't have access

Troubleshooting Info

User: legorie@gmail.com
URL: https://gcp-cookbook.appspot.com/

If you should have access, please contact
▮▮▮ ▮ ▮▮ ▮▮ ▮▮ ▮▮▮ and provide the
troubleshooting info above.

If you're signed in with multiple Google
accounts, try a different account.

6. The access denial is normal as we have not provided access to anyone in our IAP. In the IAP screen, click on the **ADD** button on the right side access pane.

7. You can add a Google account email, a Google group, a service account, or a Google Apps domain. For testing, let's add a Gmail or a G Suite account in order to access our GCP resources:

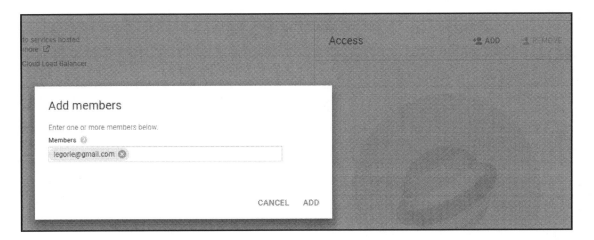

8. This adds the account to the access-allowed member list:

9. Navigate to the URL of the App Engine and you'll be able to view the application with the user account shown in the preceding screenshot:

10. Without adding authentication into the application, we are now able to control access to our App Engine application using the Identity-Aware Proxy.

Securing financial data using Cloud KMS

Cloud KMS is GCP's key management service, which generates, rotates, and destroys AES256 encryption keys. Coupled with IAM and Cloud Audit Logging, we can provide granular access at a key level and monitor their usage. We can use the KMS feature via API calls and client libraries for different languages. In this recipe, we'll use KMS to encrypt a small piece of sensitive data using Google's command-line tools. This will show us the ease of use of Cloud KMS and the absence of any overhead of managing keys or encryption libraries.

Getting ready

The following are the initial setup verification steps, which are required before the recipe can be executed:

1. Create or select a GCP project.
2. Enable billing and enable the default APIs (some APIs like BigQuery, storage, monitoring, and a few others are enabled automatically).
3. Enable the KMS API for the project you have selected:

```
gcloud services enable cloudkms.googleapis.com
```

How to do it...

This recipe will be of two parts. The first part is to set up the Cloud KMS key, which will be part of a keyring. Then, we'll use the generated key to encrypt and decrypt our secret data. For the secret data, let us take a sensitive financial data for a *credit card: 1234 4321 2342 9084* and save it to a text file. We'll use the key generated to encrypt the file and push the encrypted file to be stored on a public data store, for this we'll use a Google Storage bucket. Later, we can pull the encrypted file and use the KMS key to decrypt the data:

1. First, let us create a keyring called `fin-keyring`:

```
gcloud kms keyrings create fin-keyring --location global
```

2. With the `fin-keyring`, create a key named `fin-encrypt-key`:

```
gcloud kms keys create fin-encrypt-key --location global --keyring
fin-keyring --purpose encryption
```

3. The keys can be viewed by navigating to the submenu **Encryption keys** under **IAM & Admin**:

4. To find out the complete name and metadata of the key, use the `list` option of the `kms keys` subcommand:

```
$gcloud kms keys list --location global --keyring fin-keyring
NAME PURPOSE LABELS PRIMARY_ID PRIMARY_STATE
projects/<Project ID>/locations/global/keyRings/fin-
keyring/cryptoKeys/fin-encrypt-key ENCRYPT_DECRYPT 1 ENABLED
```

5. Now that we have completed the KMS setup/key creation, we'll perform the encryption and decryption of our sensitive data. Write the sensitive data, encoded using Base64 encoding, to a text file:

```
$ echo "Credit card : 1234 4321 2342 9084" | base64 > sensitive.txt
$ cat sensitive.txt
Q3JlZGl0IGNhcmQgOiAxMjM0IDQzMjEgMjM0MiA5MDg0Cg==
```

6. Encrypt the `sensitive.txt` file using the key `fin-encrypt-key`:

```
$ gcloud kms encrypt \
    --location=global  \
    --keyring=fin-keyring \
    --key=fin-encrypt-key \
    --version=1 \
    --plaintext-file=sensitive.txt \
    --ciphertext-file=encrypted.enc
```

7. Now, you can safely store the encrypted content in Google Storage:

```
$ gsutil cp encrypted.enc gs://bank-payments/
```

8. When we need to retrieve the credit card data, we can bring the encrypted file from the Google Storage to a local filesystem:

```
$ gsutil cp gs://bank-payments/encrypted.enc tobeDecrypted.enc
```

9. We can decrypt the message using the same key that was used to encrypt the data:

```
$ gcloud kms decrypt \
    --location=global \
    --keyring=fin-keyring \
    --key=fin-encrypt-key \
    --ciphertext-file=tobeDecrypted.enc \
    --plaintext-file=decrypted.dec
```

10. By decoding the Base64-encoded content, we'll be able to see the plain text sensitive data:

```
$ cat decrypted.dec | base64 --decode
Credit card : 1234 4321 2342 9084
```

Using Data Loss Prevention API

The DLP API is a service from GCP which understands raw data and identifies sensitive data. In addition to its ability to identify, the DLP API can also redact sensitive data. There are more than 50 detectors handled by the API and it can classify both text and images streams from applications and storage systems. The DLP API is designed to handle the **General Data Protection Regulation (GDPR)** and other compliance requirements of an application. This recipe gives you hands-on usage of the DLP API via a Python program.

Getting ready

The following are the initial setup verification steps, which are required before the recipe can be executed:

1. Create or select a GCP project.
2. Enable billing and enable the default APIs (some APIs like BigQuery, storage, monitoring, and a few others are enabled automatically).
3. Enable the DLP API for the project you have selected. Navigate to **APIs & Services**, search for DLP, and enable it.

How to do it...

In this recipe, we take an input `data.csv` which has some sensitive data. A Python program parses the file and generates a request JSON file for the API. The second part of the same Python program validates the response and gives a custom output to the user:

1. Navigate to the `Chapter04/using_dlp_api` folder.

2. The Python program `check-with-dlp.py` reads the data from the `data.csv` file and generates a request. The request is sent to the DLP API and the response is parsed to find if there is sensitive information in the data sent. The first part of the code is the initial setup for the program:

```
# -*- coding: utf-8 -*-
"""
@author: Legorie
# The code identifies sensitive information and logs it on the
console
"""
import json
import requests

# Enter the API Key which has access to the DLP API
api_key = "<Enter API Key>"
```

3. Then, we have a function to verify the likelihood of the response return from the DLP API. The API returns six types of match likelihood namely `LIKELIHOOD_UNSPECIFIED`, `VERY_UNLIKELY`, `UNLIKELY`, `POSSIBLE`, `LIKELY`, and `VERY_LIKELY`.

```
# Functions returns true if the likelihood is acceptable
def verify_likelihood(match):
    if match in ['POSSIBLE','LIKELY','VERY_LIKELY']:
        return 1
    else:
        return 0
```

4. The `main()` function can be divided into two parts. The first part reads the data from the input file, line by line. The JSON request is built using the JSON module. We are building the request for phone number and email address verification in the given text:

```
with open('data.csv') as txtfile:
    for line in txtfile:
        #print(line)
        line_num+=1
```

```
data['item'] = {}
data['item']['type'] = 'text/plain'
data['item']['value'] = line
data['inspectConfig'] = {}
data['inspectConfig']['infoTypes'] = []
pNum = {}
pNum['name'] = 'PHONE_NUMBER'
data['inspectConfig']['infoTypes'].append(pNum)
eMail = {}
eMail['name'] = 'EMAIL_ADDRESS'
data['inspectConfig']['infoTypes'].append(eMail)
json_data = json.dumps(data)
```

Print the variable json_data to have a look at the request JSON sent to the API.

5. The built JSON data is sent to the DLP API using appropriate authentication and the response is collected:

```
r = requests.post('https://dlp.googleapis.com/v2beta2/projects/
<Project ID>/content:inspect?key=' + api_key, data=json_data)
#print(r.status_code)
response = r.json()
```

6. The response is then validated to check if an acceptable likelihood is achieved for the requested line item:

```
if 'findings' in response['result']:
    if len(response['result']['findings']) == 2 and \
        verify_likelihood(response['result']['findings'][0]
        ['likelihood']) and \
        verify_likelihood(response['result']['findings'][1]
        ['likelihood']):
    #if response['result']['findings']['infoType']['name'] ==
    'PHONE_NUMBER':
        print("Phone number and Email address are present in line #"
        + str(line_num))
    elif response['result']['findings'][0]['infoType']['name'] ==
    'PHONE_NUMBER' and \
        verify_likelihood(response['result']['findings'][0]
        ['likelihood']):
        print("Phone number is present in line #" + str(line_num))
    elif response['result']['findings'][0]['infoType']['name'] ==
    'EMAIL_ADDRESS' and \
        verify_likelihood(response['result']['findings'][0]
```

```
                    ['likelihood']):
            print("Email address is present in line #" + str(line_num))
```

The results are then logged on the Console. The following is example test data:

```
First Name, Last Name, Address, Mobile, email, Credit Card
Robert, Bernista, '232, 95th Street, Wisconsin', +001-142-232-2387,
testo@example.com, 9374 7363 8273 3943
John, Shuman, '555 W Madison, Chicago', +001-312-223-3212,
legorie@gmail.com, 7363 3637 2983 3234
John, Shuman, '555 W Madison, Chicago', +001-312-223-3212, , 7363
3637 2983 3234
Robert, Bernista, '232, 95th Street, Wisconsin', , testo@example,
9374 7363 8273 3943
Bernie, Sanman, '232, 95th Street, Wisconsin', , testo@example.com,
9374 7363 8273 3943
```

The following is the output of the preceding data:

```
Phone number and Email address are present in line #2
Phone number and Email address are present in line #3
Phone number is present in line #4
Email address is present in line #6
```

Creating IAM custom roles

A group of permissions that can be assigned to a user, group, or a service account is called a **role**. In GCP, permissions for user resources cannot be directly assigned to users; they will have to grant those permissions to a role and attach the role to the user. There are three broad classifications of roles: primitive roles, predefined roles, and custom roles.

Primitive roles are viewer, editor, and owner roles, which have a broad usage and can be assigned at the project level. The predefined roles come into play when we need more fine-grained permissions. A user can be assigned to be an editor of a service, viewer of a service, a viewer plus editor of only one action, and so on. Multiple predefined roles can be assigned to a user. When the existing primitive roles do not suffice the business needs of an organization, GCP offers to create custom roles for us. With custom roles, we can go to the highest level of granularity provided by IAM. We can pick and choose the list of permissions for a role and create a custom role.

In this recipe, we'll create a custom role for a storage reviewer. A storage reviewer is someone who reviews the work of the storage admin and provides feedback. As he/she is an external reviewer, we'll not provide any editor access to the storage resource.

Getting ready

The following are the initial setup verification steps, which are required before the recipe can be executed:

1. Create or select a GCP project.
2. Enable billing and enable the default APIs (some APIs like BigQuery, storage, monitoring, and a few others are enabled automatically).
3. Appropriate permission to create a custom user role must have the `iam.roles.create` permission. Users with an organization-level administrator role or an IAM role administrator role will be able to create custom roles.

How to do it...

Our requirement is to create a storage reviewer role for compute resource, who reviews the work of a Compute Storage Admin. To start with, we can take the predefined role of `roles/compute.storageAdmin` as a base and fine-tune the permissions for the reviewer role:

1. Log in to the console and launch the Google Cloud Shell:
2. Let's find out the permissions assigned to the `roles/compute.storageAdmin` from its metadata:

```
$ gcloud beta iam roles describe roles/compute.storageAdmin
description: Full control of Compute Engine storage resources.
etag: AA==
includedPermissions:
- compute.diskTypes.get
- compute.diskTypes.list
- compute.disks.create
- compute.disks.createSnapshot
- compute.disks.delete
- compute.disks.get
- compute.disks.getIamPolicy
- compute.disks.list
- compute.disks.resize
- compute.disks.setIamPolicy
- compute.disks.setLabels
- compute.disks.update
- compute.snapshots.create
- compute.disks.use
- compute.disks.useReadOnly
- compute.globalOperations.get
```

```
- compute.globalOperations.list
- compute.images.create
- compute.images.delete
- compute.images.deprecate
- compute.images.get
- compute.images.getFromFamily
- compute.images.getIamPolicy
- compute.images.list
- compute.images.setIamPolicy
- compute.images.setLabels
- compute.images.update
- compute.images.useReadOnly
- compute.licenseCodes.get
- compute.licenseCodes.list
- compute.licenseCodes.update
- compute.licenseCodes.use
- compute.licenses.create
- compute.licenses.get
- compute.licenses.getIamPolicy
- compute.licenses.list
- compute.licenses.setIamPolicy
- compute.projects.get
- compute.regionOperations.get
- compute.regionOperations.list
- compute.regions.get
- compute.regions.list
- compute.snapshots.create
- compute.snapshots.delete
- compute.snapshots.get
- compute.snapshots.getIamPolicy
- compute.snapshots.list
- compute.snapshots.setIamPolicy
- compute.snapshots.setLabels
- compute.snapshots.useReadOnly
- compute.zoneOperations.get
- compute.zoneOperations.list
- compute.zones.get
- compute.zones.list
- resourcemanager.projects.get
- resourcemanager.projects.list
- serviceusage.quotas.get
- serviceusage.services.get
name: roles/compute.storageAdmin
stage: GA
title: Compute Storage Admin
```

3. Copy the included permissions to a separate text file and remove all the permissions related to `create/delete/update/resize`. Leave only the read-only permission for the reviewer. We'll use this permission list later in the recipe.

4. To create a custom role, we'll need to prepare a YAML file with the following format:

```
title: [ROLE_TITLE]
description: [ROLE_DESCRIPTION]
stage: [LAUNCH_STAGE]
includedPermissions:
- [PERMISSION_1]
- [PERMISSION_2]
```

5. Enter an appropriate title and description for the role to be created. The stage indicates the life cycle of the custom role as ALPHA, BETA, or GA. Also, use the list of permissions selected in *Step 3* in the `includedPermissions` section:

storageReviewer.yaml

```
title: Storage Reviewer
description: Role for Storage Reviewer
stage: ALPHA
includedPermissions:
- compute.diskTypes.get
- compute.diskTypes.list
- compute.disks.get
- compute.disks.list
- compute.disks.useReadOnly
- compute.globalOperations.get
- compute.globalOperations.list
- compute.images.get
- compute.images.getFromFamily
- compute.images.list
- compute.images.useReadOnly
- compute.projects.get
- compute.regionOperations.get
- compute.regionOperations.list
- compute.regions.get
- compute.regions.list
- compute.snapshots.get
- compute.snapshots.list
- compute.snapshots.useReadOnly
- compute.zoneOperations.get
- compute.zoneOperations.list
```

```
- compute.zones.get
- compute.zones.list
- resourcemanager.projects.get
```

6. To create the custom role, we can use the following command:

```
$ gcloud beta iam roles create compute.storageReviewer
--project <Project ID> --file storageReview.yaml
```

7. Navigate to **IAM & Admin** and to the **Roles** submenu to view the created **Storage Reviewer** customrole:

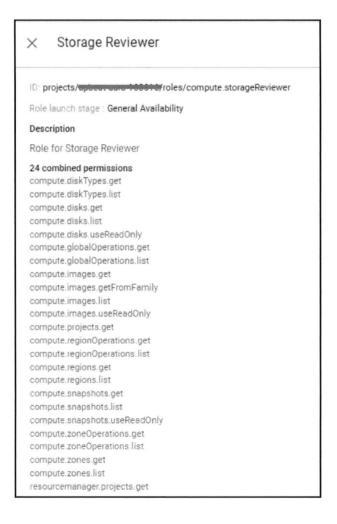

8. To test the custom role, we can now assign this custom role to a user and test their access. Before the custom role can be assigned to a user, the custom role should move to a **General Availability** status. So, edit the `compute.storageReviewer` role and update the **Role launch stage**:

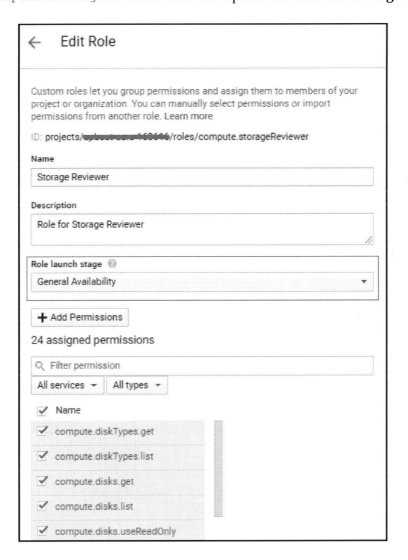

9. Navigate to **IAM** and click on **ADD**. Enter the member's details and select the **Storage Reviewer** from the **Custom** role section:

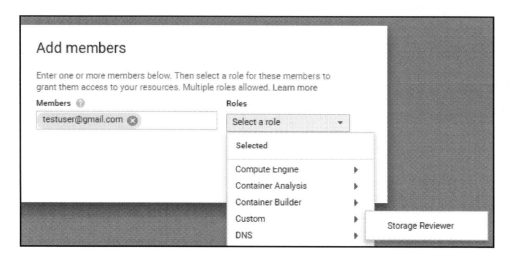

10. Log in to the GCP Console with the member's details and verify that you have access to review the storage details in the compute service.

11. Refer to the following screenshot to view access:

12. Refer to the following screenshot to create access denial:

Creating service accounts

A service account is a non-user account generated by the GCP for services or manually created for our applications. When a service account is attached to an application, it assumes the identity of the service account and thus avoids storing credentials at the application level. The services which can be accessed by the service account can be managed via IAM.

In addition to applications assuming the service account's access, users can also use the service account to access resources. In this recipe, we'll create a service account and use it to verify access to Cloud SQL.

Getting ready

The following are the initial setup verification steps, which are required before the recipe can be executed:

1. Create or select a GCP project.
2. Enable billing and enable the default APIs (some APIs like BigQuery, storage, monitoring, and a few others are enabled automatically).
3. Give a appropriate permission to create service accounts.
4. Verify that the Google Cloud SQL API is enabled.

5. Let us also create a Cloud SQL instance to test our service accounts:
    1. Navigate to the **SQL** submenu and click on **Create instance**.
    2. Select MySQL as your database engine and choose the latest generation.
    3. Give an **Instance ID** and a password.
    4. With the defaults, create a Cloud SQL instance:

	Instance ID	Type	IP address	Instance connection name
	mysql-test	MySQL 2nd Gen 5.7	35.192.104.137	upbeat-aura-163616:us-central1:mysql-test

How to do it...

We'll first create a service account with default access rights. Next, we'll launch a VM with the newly created service account. Ideally, the VM would not have direct access to Cloud SQL. Then, in IAM we'll assign the Cloud SQL admin rights to our service account and redo our verification:

1. Launch the Google Cloud Shell from the Console:

2. We'll create a service account using the following command:

```
$ gcloud iam service-accounts create my-sa-with-sql --display-name
"Service a/c with sql access"
```

3. To view all the service accounts, we can use the following command:

```
$ gcloud iam service-accounts list
```

```
NAME                          EMAIL
Service a/c with sql access   my-sa-with-sql@upbeat-
aura-163616.iam.gserviceaccount.com
```

The following screenshot shows the output for the preceding command:

4. Now, we'll launch a VM with our newly created service account:

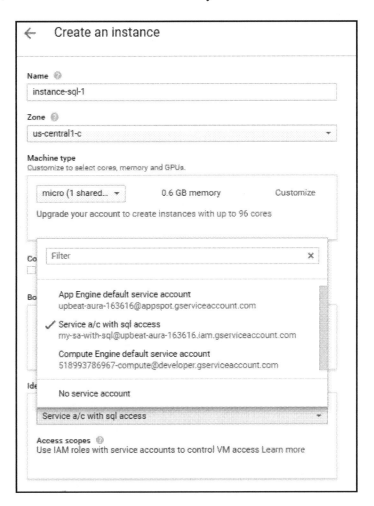

5. SSH into the instance we have created and install a MySQL client which can be used by the `gcloud` command:

```
$ sudo apt install mysql-client
```

6. From the instance, try to connect to our Cloud SQL instance. Ideally, you'll get an error reaching the SQL service:

```
$ gcloud sql connect mysql-test --user=root

ERROR: (gcloud.sql.connect) HTTPError 403: The client is not
authorized to make this request.
```

7. Next, we'll go to the IAM Console and click on **ADD**:

8. Enter the service account ID in the **Members** textbox, select the **Cloud SQL Admin** role, and click on the **Add** button:

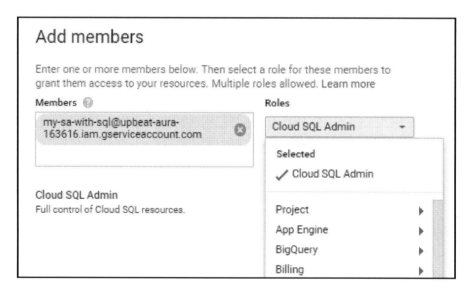

9. Navigate the SSH window of our instance and rerun the `gcloud sql` command. This time, the VM should have access to connect to the Cloud SQL service:

```
instance-sql-1:~$ gcloud sql connect mysql-test --user=root
ERROR: (gcloud.sql.connect) HTTPError 403: The client is not authorized to make this request.
instance-sql-1:~$ gcloud sql connect mysql-test --user=root
Whitelisting your IP for incoming connection for 5 minutes...done.
Connecting to database with SQL user [root].Enter password:
Welcome to the MariaDB monitor.  Commands end with ; or \g.
Your MySQL connection id is 434
Server version: 5.7.14-google-log (Google)

Copyright (c) 2000, 2017, Oracle, MariaDB Corporation Ab and others.

Type 'help;' or '\h' for help. Type '\c' to clear the current input statement.

MySQL [(none)]>
```

Automatic recon and defense

"Automating security" has been a buzzphrase in the world of information security since the dawn of Cloud. It refers to a wide range of products which provide security by monitoring logs and bringing intelligence into processing. The Google Cloud APIs provide us with a plethora of options to monitor and take actions programmatically against events.

For this recipe, let us suppose that someone has compromised our programmatic access to GCP and has started launching unauthorized instances in our project. We'll need a way to identify such incidents and take defensive action against such events. We'll make some assumptions as follows:

- Regular users of the account are allowed only to create `g1-small` and `n1-standard` machines
- The controls on user access for the above are set using IAM, which are not covered as part of this recipe
- The authority under which the Python program will run is not compromised; that is, the authority exists on a different security plane than that of the plane of the possible attack

Getting ready

Following are the initial setup verification steps to take before the recipe can be executed:

1. Create or select a GCP project
2. Enable billing and enable the default APIs (some APIs like BigQuery, storage, monitoring, and a few others are enabled automatically)
3. Verify that the monitoring and logging APIs are enabled for the project
4. Verify that the development machine has the credentials necessary to execute GCP APIs

How to do it...

To set up our unauthorized activity alerting system, we'll create a Python program that will first verify the logs to find out if there are any unauthorized machines are created. If any unauthorized machine identified, the program will proceed to terminate them:

1. In the *Creating alerts on specific events* recipe in `Chapter 6`, *Management Tools*, you'll find how to filter logs and focus on the events which interest us. Similarly, for our security situation, we are interested in instances created and their instance type. The following is an example of a log filter:

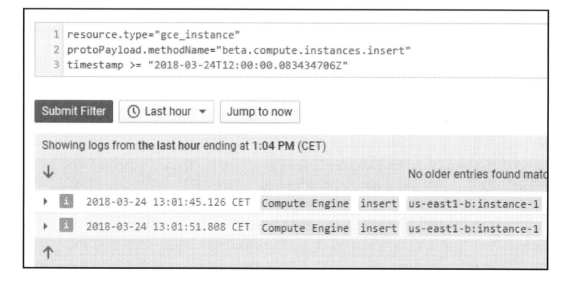

2. Next, we'll have to convert this log filter into an API request. Navigate to Google's API-explorer, `https://developers.google.com/apis-explorer/`, in your favorite browser and select the **Stackdriver Logging API**:

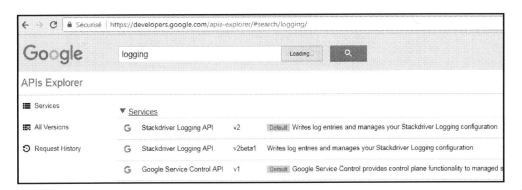

3. Select the `logging.entries.list` API, which will suit our requirements:

logging.entries.list — Lists log entries. Use this method to retrieve log entries from Stackdriver Logging. For ways to export log entries, see Exporting Logs.

4. We'll now have to transform the log filter used in the *step 1* to an API request format. You can use the *structured editor* to create the request body of the API:

5. The following is request body in text format:

```
{
   "resourceNames":
   [
      "projects/gcp-cookbook"
   ],
   "filter": "logName=projects/gcp-
               cookbook/logs/cloudaudit.googleapis.com%2Factivity AND
               resource.type=gce_instance AND
               \nprotoPayload.methodName=beta.compute.instances
               .insert AND
               operation.first=True AND \ntimestamp >= \
               "2018-01-24T02:13:02.356425Z\""
}
```

6. You can authorize and test the API request to the `logging.entries.list` API and view the output response:

```
logging.entries.list executed moments ago   time to execute: 484 ms

Request

POST https://logging.googleapis.com/v2/entries:list?key={YOUR_API_KEY}
-{
 -"resourceNames": [
    "projects/gcp-cookbook"
  ],
  "filter": "logName=projects/gcp-cookbook/logs/cloudaudit.googleapis.com%2Factivity AND \nresource.type=gce_instance AND
\nprotoPayload.methodName=beta.compute.instances.insert AND \noperation.first=True AND \ntimestamp >= \"2018-03-24T02:13:02.356425Z\""
 }

Response

200
- Show headers -
-{
 -"entries": [
  -{
   -"protoPayload": {
      "@type": "type.googleapis.com/google.cloud.audit.AuditLog",
     -"authenticationInfo": {
```

7. Now, we'll use this API request in the Python program. Navigate to
   `Chapter04/autosecurity` to view the program:

```python
def check_logs(project_id):
    # Checks the logs for the creation event of an instance using
    filters & processes the response
    credentials = GoogleCredentials.get_application_default()
    service = build('logging', 'v2', credentials=credentials)

    req_body = { "resourceNames": ["projects/"+ project_id],
                 "filter": 'logName=projects/'+ project_id +
                            '/logs/cloudaudit.googleapis.com
                            %2Factivity AND'
                            'resource.type=gce_instance AND
                            protoPayload.methodName=beta.compute
                            .instances.insert AND '
                            'operation.first=True AND '
                            'timestamp >= "' + get_start_time() + '"'
                }
    collection = service.entries()
    request = collection.list(body=req_body)
    response = request.execute()
    #print(response)
    #print('----')
    if response != {} :
        for res in response['entries']:
            print(res)
            mctype = res['protoPayload']['request']
            ['machineType'].split('/')
            user = res['protoPayload']['authenticationInfo']
            ['principalEmail']
            instance = res['protoPayload']
            ['resourceName'].split('/')
            zone = res['resource']['labels']['zone']
            print(mctype[-1], user, instance[-1])
            verify_mctype_kill(mctype[-1], user, instance[-1],
            zone, project_id)
    else:
        print('No instance creation activity found.')
```

8. The preceding function constructs the request body for what to request of the
   API. Once the API returns the result, it processes the response. If there is a
   response, then the next function is for calling for verification and for taking
   action.

9. The allowed machine types are defined in the following function. When the machine type of the instance created is not in one of the allowed machine types, the machine is deleted. Since there are chances that old logs will be processed again, we invoke the compute API to make sure that the instance is present:

```
def verify_mctype_kill(machine, user, instance_name, zone,
project):
    # A * to indicate the NOT allowed machine types
    allowed_machines = ['*f1-micro','g1-small', 'n1-standard',
    '*n1-highmem', '*n1-highcpu', '*n1-megamem']
    mc_split = machine.split('-')
    if len(mc_split) == 3:
        mc_split.pop()
    mc_type = '-'.join(mc_split)

    if mc_type not in allowed_machines:
        print(instance_name + ' has a machine type of ' + mc_type
        + ' which is not an allowed.')
        compute = googleapiclient.discovery.build('compute', 'v1')
        print("Verifying if machine is present ... "
        + instance_name)
        try:
            request  = compute.instances().get(project=project_id,
            zone=zone, instance=instance_name)
            response = request.execute()
        except HttpError as err:
            # If the error is a rate limit or connection error,
            # wait and try again.
            if err.resp.status in [404]:
                print("Instance not found")
                return
            else: raise
        print('Deleting instance ' + instance_name)
        op = delete_instance(compute, project_id, zone,
        instance_name)
        wait_for_operation(compute, project, zone, op['name'])
```

10. The following are some of the supporting functions to help the execution of the previously discussed functions:

```
def format_rfc3339(datetime_instance=None):
    """Formats a datetime per RFC 3339.
    :param datetime_instance: Datetime instance to format, defaults
    to utcnow
    """

    return datetime_instance.isoformat("T") + "Z"
```

```
def get_start_time():
    # Return now- 5 minutes
    start_time = datetime.datetime.utcnow() -
    datetime.timedelta(minutes=600)
    return format_rfc3339(start_time)


def get_now_rfc3339():
    # Return now
    return format_rfc3339(datetime.datetime.utcnow())

def wait_for_operation(compute, project, zone, operation):
    print('Waiting for operation to finish...')
    while True:
        result = compute.zoneOperations().get(
            project=project,
            zone=zone,
            operation=operation).execute()

        if result['status'] == 'DONE':
            print("done.")
            if 'error' in result:
                raise Exception(result['error'])
            return result

        time.sleep(1)

def delete_instance(compute, project, zone, name):
    return compute.instances().delete(
        project=project,
        zone=zone,
        instance=name).execute()
```

11. Install the required Python packages and ensure that the
    GOOGLE_APPLICATION_CREDENTIALS is properly set. The program uses the
    Application Default Credentials (ADC) strategy to communicate with the API:

```
$ virtualenv env
$ source env/bin/activate
$ pip install -r requirements
$ python autosec-api.py <Project ID>
No instance creation activity found.
```

12. Now, let us create an `f1-micro` instance under the project and run the program again.

```
$ python autosec-api.py <Project ID>
instance-1 has a machine type of f1-micro which is not an allowed.
Verify if machine is present instance-1
Deleting instance instance-1
Waiting for operation to finish...
done.
```

5
Machine Learning and Big Data

In this chapter, we will cover:

- Uploading data to the Google BigQuery table
- Translating text to a target language
- Creating a Dataflow pipeline to store streaming data
- Using the Vision API
- Using the Google Cloud Speech API
- Using the Cloud IoT Core

Introduction

In this chapter, we'll discover Google Cloud's offering on **machine learning** (**ML**) and a few big data services. GCP offers two kinds of ML platform—one where we can use our own data to train models using services like Cloud ML Engine, and another to use already trained ML models for specific use cases like that of Cloud Natural Language, Translation API, Vision API, Speech API, and Video Intelligence. We'll focus more on machine learning APIs in this chapter.

GCP provides a wide range of services for end to end big data processing, of which we'll look at three services in particular—Google BigQuery, Cloud Dataflow, and Pub/Sub.

One of the biggest strengths of GCP is their big data services and ML capabilities. The technology behind these services existed in Google even before the arrival of the public cloud.

Uploading data to the Google BigQuery table

Google BigQuery is a petabyte scale, serverless, low cost data analytics service. The ability to use standard SQL is one of the great advantages from a developer standpoint. BigQuery uses columnar storage, massively parallel processing, and performance adjustments for the data processing of large datasets.

In this recipe, we'll learn to insert data into a BigQuery table continuously and later query it from the web interface.

Getting ready

The following steps are the initial setup verification steps for the creation of the network before the recipe can be executed:

1. Create or select a GCP project
2. Enable billing and enable the default APIs (some APIs like BigQuery, storage, monitoring, and a few others are enabled automatically)

How to do it...

In this recipe, we'll extract some data from Twitter using the Twitter API and load it into a BigQuery table. Once the data is loaded, we'll use the web interface to query the stored items:

1. Navigate to the BigQuery home page and select your GCP project: `https://bigquery.cloud.google.com/`.
2. Next, let's create a new dataset called `TwitterData` and a table called `theTweets`, to hold the extracted data:

3. While creating the table, add two columns, screen_name and tweet_txt:

4. Once the BigQuery setup has been completed, navigate to the `Chapter05/data2BQ` folder.

5. To execute the program in an isolated environment, create a `virtualenv` and install the dependent packages:

```
$ virtualenv ENV
$ source ENV/bin/activate
$ pip install -r requirements.txt
```

The following is the contents of the `requirements.txt` file:

```
google-cloud-bigquery==0.31.0
tweepy==3.6.0
```

6. The Python code extracts data from Twitter and pushes each message into the BigQuery table which we created.

7. The client libraries are successfully imported. We'll use the Tweepy Python library to extract data from Twitter:

```
import json
import argparse

#Import the necessary methods from tweepy library
from tweepy.streaming import StreamListener
from tweepy import OAuthHandler
from tweepy import Stream

from google.cloud import bigquery
```

8. The access keys that use the Twitter API are hardcoded:

```
### Hardcoding tokens in a program is never a good idea. This can be used only for
learning ###
access_token = ""
access_token_secret = ""
consumer_key = ""
consumer_secret = ""
```

The tokens to communicate with Twitter have to be generated by creating a Twitter app, which you can learn more about here: `https://developer.twitter.com/en/docs/basics/authentication/guides/access-tokens`.

9. The BigQuery dataset and table created in the previous steps are hardcoded as follows:

```
#Hardcoded values for BigQuery
bq_dataset_name = "TwitterData"
bq_table_name = "theTweets"
project_id = ""
```

10. The `upload_bigQuery` function receives the Twitter screen name and Twitter text data and inserts them into the table:

```
def upload_bigQuery(name, text):
    bigquery_client = bigquery.Client(project=project_id)
    dataset_ref = bigquery_client.dataset(bq_dataset_name)
    table_ref = dataset_ref.table(bq_table_name)

    # Get the table from the API so that the schema is available.
    table = bigquery_client.get_table(table_ref)

    rows_to_insert = [
      (name, text)
    ]

    errors = bigquery_client.create_rows(table, rows_to_insert)
    # API request

    if not errors:
        print('Loaded 1 row into table')
    else:
        print('Errors:')
        print(errors)
```

11. Using Tweepy's `StreamListener`, you can use the Twitter streaming API and download messages in real time. The downloaded JSON data is parsed, and the screen name and text are sent to the BigQuery table. In the main part of the code, the program expects the GCP project ID to be an argument:

```
class StdOutListener(StreamListener):

    def on_data(self, data):
        jdata = json.loads(data)
        print(jdata['user']['screen_name'], jdata['text'])
        upload_bigQuery(jdata['user']['screen_name'],
jdata['text'])
        print("========")
        return True
```

```
    def on_error(self, status):
        print(status)


if __name__ == '__main__':
    parser = argparse.ArgumentParser(
    description=__doc__,
    formatter_class=argparse.ArgumentDefaultsHelpFormatter)
    parser.add_argument('project_id', help='Your Cloud Platform
    project ID.')

    args = parser.parse_args()
    project_id = args.project_id

    l = StdOutListener()
    auth = OAuthHandler(consumer_key, consumer_secret)
    auth.set_access_token(access_token, access_token_secret)
    stream = Stream(auth, l)
    stream.filter(track=['GCP','Google Cloud'])
```

12. After installing all the required Python packages, with the proper API access keys and having access to the BigQuery API, the code will insert data as expected. The program streams continuously, but you can stop the code using *Ctrl + C* when you have enough tweets displayed on the standard Console:

    $ python twitter2BQ.py <Project ID>

    The output of the preceding command can be seen in the following screenshot:

The data can be queried from the BigQuery table as below:

There's more...

In addition to querying via the web interface, BigQuery data can be queried by using the command line, and API calls, and via client SDKs. There are two modes to execute the queries— interactive mode and batch mode.

In the interactive mode, the queries are executed immediately whereas, in the batch mode, the queries are queued to be processed when resources become available. By waiting for available resources, batch queries do not count toward the concurrent rate limit and daily limit.

The following is an example of the command-line query in interactive and batch modes:

```
$ bq query  "SELECT screen_name FROM [<Project ID>:TwitterData.theTweets]
LIMIT 1000"

Waiting on bqjob_r6e562a9ffa61eb18_00000161fd61f724_1 ... (0s) Current
status: DONE
+----------------+
|  screen_name   |
+----------------+
| xxxxxx         |
| xxxxxxxx       |
| xxxxxxxxxxx    |
| xxxxxxxx       |
| xxxxxxx        |
| xxxxxxxxx      |
```

```
|  xxxxxxxxx     |
+---------------+

$ bq query --batch "SELECT screen_name FROM [<Project
ID>:TwitterData.theTweets] LIMIT 1000"
Waiting on bqjob_r20f56486b3cd6be_00000161fd5ba4dc_1 ... (110s) Current
status: DONE
+---------------+
|  screen_name  |
+---------------+
|  xxxxxx       |
|  xxxxxxxx     |
|  xxxxxxxxxxx  |
|  xxxxxxxx     |
+---------------+
|  xxxxxxx      |
|  xxxxxxxxx    |
|  xxxxxxxxx    |
+---------------+
```

Translating text to a target language

The Google Translation API is a machine translation service which uses a state-of-the-art neural machine translator. The service can be invoked using RESTful API calls from various programming languages. With a given text, we can invoke the API to identify the source language and we can translate to a target language of our choice. Like any other GCP service, this API is highly scalable and comes with a simple pricing model.

Getting ready

The following are the initial setup verification steps for the creation of the network before the recipe can be executed:

1. Create or select a GCP project
2. Enable billing and enable the default APIs (some APIs like BigQuery, storage, monitoring, and a few others are enabled automatically)
3. Enable the Google Cloud Translation API for your project

How to do it...

In this recipe, similar to the previous one, we'll extract some data from Twitter using the Twitter API. When the tweets are received as a stream, the Translation API is called to identify the language of the tweet. If the tweet is not in our target language, we will invoke the Translation API to perform the translation:

1. Navigate to the `Chapter05/translateTweets` folder.

2. To execute the program in an isolated environment, create a `virtualenv` and install the dependent packages:

   ```
   $ virtualenv ENV
   $ source ENV/bin/activate
   $ pip install -r requirements.txt
   ```

   The following is the contents of the `requirements.txt` file:

   ```
   google-cloud-translate==1.3.0
   tweepy==3.6.0
   ```

3. The Python code extracts data from Twitter and invokes the Translation API for language detection and translation.

4. The client libraries are imported:

   ```
   import json
   import argparse

   #Import the necessary methods from tweepy library
   from tweepy.streaming import StreamListener
   from tweepy import OAuthHandler
   from tweepy import Stream

   from google.cloud import translate
   ```

5. The access keys using the Twitter API are hardcoded:

   ```
   ### Hardcoding tokens in a program is never a good idea. This can
   be used only for learning ###
   access_token = ""
   access_token_secret = ""
   consumer_key = ""
   consumer_secret = ""
   ```

6. The `detect_translate` function receives the tweet and performs two operations:

   - The `detect` method of the Translation API is invoked to determine the language of the tweet.
   - If the detected language is not equal to `target_lang`, the `translate` method is invoked to perform the translation:

```
def detect_translate(text, target_lang):
    translate_client = translate.Client()

    # Send the tweet text to the API and detects the
language
    result = translate_client.detect_language(text)

    print(u'Tweet Text: {}'.format(text))
    print('Language: {}'.format(result['language']))

    # Checks if the detected language is in the target
language
    # else the translation API is invoked to get the text
translated
    if result['language'] != target_lang :
        translation = translate_client.translate(text,
            target_language=target_lang)
        print(u'Translation:
{}'.format(translation['translatedText']))
```

7. Using Tweepy's `StreamListener`, you can use the Twitter streaming API and download messages in real time. The downloaded JSON data is parsed and the `detect_translate` function is invoked:

```
class StdOutListener(StreamListener):

    def on_data(self, data):
        jdata = json.loads(data)
        #print(jdata['text'])
        detect_translate(jdata['text'], target_lang)
        print("------")
        return True

    def on_error(self, status):
        print(status)

if __name__ == '__main__':
    parser = argparse.ArgumentParser(
        description=__doc__,
```

```
        formatter_class=argparse.ArgumentDefaultsHelpFormatter)
        parser.add_argument('target_lang', help='Set your target
language (use iso-639-1 codes) e.g: en, fr, ru, ja')

        args = parser.parse_args()
        target_lang = args.target_lang

        #A Tweepy streaming session is instantiated to receive
        the Twitter stream
        l = StdOutListener()
        auth = OAuthHandler(consumer_key, consumer_secret)
        auth.set_access_token(access_token, access_token_secret)
        stream = Stream(auth, l)
        stream.filter(track=['news'])
```

8. After installing all the required Python packages, with the proper API access keys and access to the Translation API, the code will display the tweets in the target language:

The program streams continuously, but you can stop the code using *Ctrl + C*.

```
$ python twitter2-anyLang.py en
```

The output for the preceding command can be seen in the following screenshot:

```
Tweet Text: サッカー W 杯代表選考、2 段階で絞り込む案も ハリル監督 - 日本経済新聞 https://t.co/ZHbuum68A7 #NEWS
Language: ja
Translation: Football World Cup national team selection, also a plan to narrow down in two stages Ha Ril Director - Nihon Keizai Shimbun https://t.co/ZHbuum68A7 # NEWS
-----
Tweet Text: RT @DLoesch: From a guy that got his start being a horndog second banana on a show that ended every episode with a chick on a trampoline. H_
Language: en
-----
Tweet Text: Surprised they didn't change dates ten minutes after the news hit. https://t.co/MDGRcVN5p4
Language: en
-----
```

```
$ python twitter2-anyLang.py fr
```

The output for the preceding command can be seen in the following screenshot:

```
Tweet Text: #news #opiatecrisis #feelourpain https://t.co/eEAc54dR81
Language: en
Translation: #news #opiatecrisis #feelourpain https://t.co/eEAc54dR81
------
Tweet Text: RT @MirrorFootball: #MUFC: DE DONUT, TONI BARCELONA, Lindelof, Smalling, Young, McTominay, OTTO, Pogba, Alexis, Lukaku, Lingard https://t.c…
Language: en
Translation: RT @MirrorFootball: #MUFC: DE DONUT, TONI BARCELONE, Lindelof, Smalling, Jeune, McTominay, OTTO, Pogba, Alexis, Lukaku, Lingard https: // to ...
------
Tweet Text: High school was a learning experience for me! Nigga was all on yahoo news and all the local news stations shit was mad epic.
Language: en
Translation: Le lycée était une expérience d'apprentissage pour moi! Nigga était tout sur les nouvelles de Yahoo et toutes les merdes de stations de nouvelles
t épiques folles.
------
Tweet Text: RT @logatel3asr: #11/9/2016 يوم أهدافـي #مبـاريـات أهداف
https://t.co/7FWc4DMzn7 https://t.co/TqH7Lr08vC
Language: ar
Translation: RT @ logatel3asr: # Buts # Correspondances le 11/9/2016 https://t.co/7FWc4DMzn7 https://t.co/TqH7Lr08vC
------
Tweet Text: RT @CFMEU: "The combined strength of the CFMEU, MUA and TCFUA in our new union will write a new chapter in Australia's union movement. Ordi…
Language: en
Translation: RT @CFMEU: &quot;La force combinée du CFMEU, MUA et TCFUA dans notre nouveau syndicat va écrire un nouveau chapitre dans le mouvement syndical aus
------
Tweet Text: Google Unveils 72-Qubit Quantum Computer with Low Error Rates https://t.co/z3upUu7YqS https://t.co/Mp3m8i61r7
Language: en
Translation: Google dévoile l'ordinateur Quantum 72-Qubit avec des taux d'erreur faibles https://t.co/z3upUu7YqS https://t.co/Mp3m8i61r7
------
```

See also

If you are planning to use the Google Translation API for your applications/websites, please read the attribution requirements and HTML markup requirements in the documentation:

- https://cloud.google.com/translate/attribution
- https://cloud.google.com/translate/markup

Creating a Dataflow pipeline to store streaming data

Google Dataflow is a service for stream and batch processing at scale. When there is a need for processing lots of streamed data like click stream or data from IoT devices, Dataflow will be the starting point for receiving all the stream data. The data can then be sent to storage (BigQuery, Bigtable, GCS) for further processing (ML):

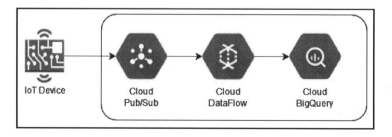

For this recipe, let's consider a weather station (IoT device) that is sending temperature data to GCP. The data is emitted constantly by the IoT device and is stored on Google Storage for later analytics processing. Considering the intermittent nature of data connectivity between the device and GCP, we'll need a solution to receive the messages, process/handle them, and store them. For this solution, we'll create a Dataflow pipeline using a Google provided template—Cloud Pub/Sub to Cloud Storage text.

Getting ready

The following are the initial setup verification steps for the creation of the network before the recipe can be executed:

1. Create or select a GCP project
2. Enable billing and enable the default APIs (some APIs like BigQuery, storage, monitoring, and a few others are enabled automatically)
3. Enable the Google Dataflow API for the project

How to do it...

To use the standard (Cloud Pub/Sub to Cloud Storage text) Dataflow template, we'll break the setup into four steps:

1. Creation of the Pub/Sub topic and subscription
2. Creating the Dataflow pipeline
3. Sending test temperature data to the Pub/Sub topic
4. Viewing the processed data and the stored data on Google Storage

Let's look into these steps in detail:

1. First, let's create a Pub/Sub topic to receive the IoT sensor's temperate data:

   ```
   $ gcloud pubsub topics create tempSensorTopic
   ```

2. Next, we'll create a subscription that can read data off the topic:

   ```
   $ gcloud pubsub subscriptions create readTempSubscptn --topic
   tempSensorTopic
   ```

3. On the GCP Console, you can view the created Pub/Sub topic and subscription:

4. The next stage is the creation of the Dataflow pipeline. Navigate to the **Dataflow** service and click on **CREATE JOB FROM TEMPLATE**:

5. Once the create form is open, enter the following details:
   1. Give a job name and select a regional endpoint.
   2. Choose the **Cloud PubSub to GCS Text** template.
   3. Provide the name of the Pub/Sub topic created in the previous step.
   4. Provide a valid storage bucket for the output and the temporary files to be written.

5. You can provide details for the other optional parameters, if necessary. A sample of the details entered is given as follows:

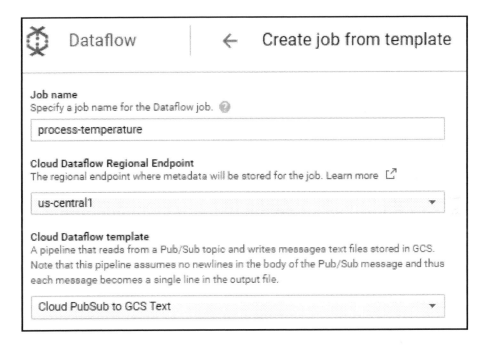

6. Fill in the information as shown in the following screenshot:

Parameters

Input Cloud Pub/Sub topic
Cloud Pub/Sub topic to read the input from. The topic name should be in the format of projects/<project-id>/topics/<topic-name>.

projects/gcp-cookbook/topics/tempSensorTopic

Output Cloud Storage directory
Path and filename prefix for writing output files (ex: gs://bucket-name/path/). This value must end in a slash.

gs://tempsensor/data/

Output file prefix
The prefix to place on each windowed file (ex: output-).

df

Output file suffix (Optional)
[Optional] The suffix to place on each windowed file. Typically a file extension (.txt, .csv, etc.).

txt

The shard template (Optional)
[Optional] The shard template defines the unique/dynamic portion of each windowed file. Recommended to use the default (W-P-SS-of-NN). At runtime, 'W' is replaced with the window date range and 'P' is replaced with the pane info. Repeating sequences of the letters 'S' or 'N' (example: SSS-NNN) are replaced with the shard number and number of shards respectively. The pipeline assumes a single file output and thus will produce the text of '00-of-01' by default.

Temporary Location
Path and filename prefix for writing temporary files. ex: gs://MyBucket/tmp

gs://tempsensor/tmp/

7. Click on **Run job** to launch the pipeline. The job will get to its running state:

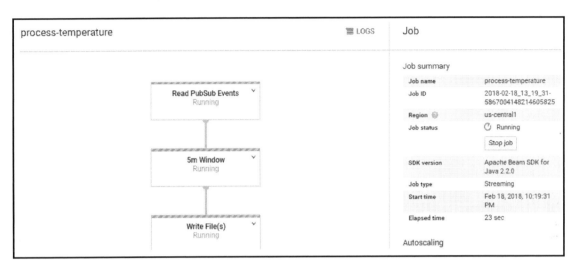

8. To trigger the pipeline, we will put some mock up temperate data into the Pub/Sub topic. From the Cloud Shell, send the following sample messages to the topic:

```
$ gcloud pubsub topics publish tempSensorTopic --message '22-
Jan-2018 10:12:43 70.0F'
$ gcloud pubsub topics publish tempSensorTopic --message '22-
Jan-2018 10:12:55 70.0F'
$ gcloud pubsub topics publish tempSensorTopic --message '22-
Jan-2018 10:13:04 70.6F'
$ gcloud pubsub topics publish tempSensorTopic --message '22-
Jan-2018 10:14:36 70.1F'
$ gcloud pubsub topics publish tempSensorTopic --message '22-
Jan-2018 10:16:20 71.0F'
```

9. From the GCP Console, you can see that the five messages are received by the different steps of the pipeline:

- Stage 1—Pub/Sub event:

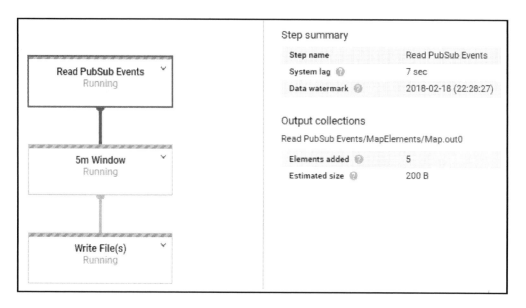

- Stage 2—processing:

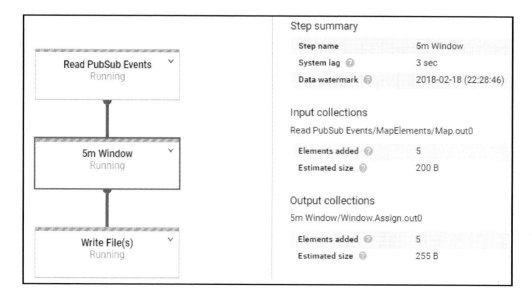

- Stage 3—writing to storage:

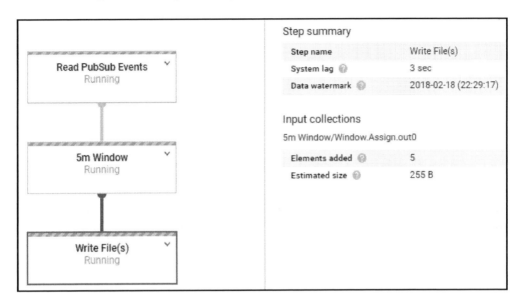

10. Once job processing is complete, you'll be able to see the output in the expected storage bucket:

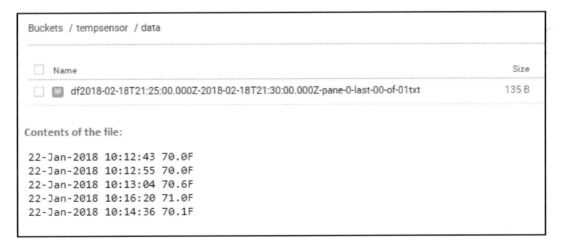

11. Make sure you stop the job once processing is completed to stop the workers and avoid unnecessary billing.

Using the Vision API

The Google Vision API is an advanced application API to perform image analysis. The salient features are:

- **Safe search**: Content moderation of an image
- **Label detection**: Reads the image and detects objects, events, locations, products and so on
- **Face detection**: Detects faces and facial features
- **Landmark detection**: Detects natural and man-made landmarks
- **OCR**: Detects text within an image
- **Logo detection**: Detects popular products and corporate logos
- **Web entities**: Detects the contents of the image and returns its information as related to the Google Knowledge Graph

We'll try a simple example of using the Vision API for uploading images to a photo field of a signup form.

Getting ready

The following are the initial setup verification steps for the creation of the network before the recipe can be executed:

1. Create or select a GCP project
2. Enable billing and enable the default APIs (some APIs like BigQuery, storage, monitoring, and a few others are enabled automatically)
3. Enable the Google Vision API for the project
4. Make sure that the code has access to GCP APIs using the Application Default Credential strategy or direct API keys

How to do it...

The code for this recipe takes an image file and verifies whether the image has a face and that it isn't a spoofed image. It makes two calls to the Vision API to determine this:

1. After cloning the source code of the book, navigate to the `Chapter05/vision-api` folder.

2. To execute the program in an isolated environment, create a `virtualenv` and install the dependent packages:

   ```
   $ virtualenv ENV
   $ source ENV/bin/activate
   $ pip install -r requirements.txt
   ```

   The following is the contents of the `requirements.txt` file:

   ```
   google-cloud-storage==1.7.0
   google-cloud-vision==0.30.0
   Pillow==5.0.0
   ```

3. The following is the program which invokes the Vision API:

   1. The client libraries are imported. We'll use the **Python Imaging Library** (**PIL**) to pass images to the Vision API:

      ```
      import argparse
      from google.cloud import storage
      from google.cloud import vision
      from google.cloud.vision import types
      from PIL import Image
      ```

   2. Create a bucket called `images` or change the following line in the code with an existing bucket name:

      ```
      bucket_id = 'images'
      ```

   3. The `upload2GCS` function simply uploads the file to Google Storage:

      ```
      def upload2GCS(project_id, file_name):
       # Uploads the images to Google Storage
       client = storage.Client(project=project_id)
       bucket = client.get_bucket(bucket_id)
       gcs_filename = "tmp" #Adding a prefix to the file name
       gcs_filename = gcs_filename + file_name
       blob2 = bucket.blob(gcs_filename)
      ```

```
blob2.upload_from_filename(filename=file_name)
return("File uploaded to GCS : ", file_name)
```

4. The `visionTest` function is the core of the program which invokes the Vision API. First, it invokes the API to determine whether there is a face in the given image. If `face_annotations` is returned, then this confirms that the image contains a face. If the result is empty, then no face has been detected and the process stops. The second check is the call to safe search detection to detect any spoofing on the image:

```
def visionTest(project_id, img_file):
 # Function verifies if the images contains a face and
is not spoofed using the Cloud Vision API

likelihood_name = ('UNKNOWN', 'VERY_UNLIKELY',
'UNLIKELY', 'POSSIBLE',
 'LIKELY', 'VERY_LIKELY')
# Names of likelihood from google.cloud.vision.enums
 vclient = vision.ImageAnnotatorClient()
 content = img_file.read()
 image = types.Image(content=content)
faceResult =
vclient.face_detection(image=image).face_annotations
 if not faceResult:
 return("Uploaded images does not contains a person's
face")
 else:
# Test for safe content
 response = vclient.safe_search_detection(image=image)
 safe = response.safe_search_annotation
if likelihood_name[safe.spoof] in ['LIKELY',
'VERY_LIKELY']:
 return('Possible spoofed image')
 else:
 return('Upload2GCS')
```

5. The `main` function just prepares the input arguments and calls the appropriate functions:

```
if __name__ == '__main__':
    parser = argparse.ArgumentParser(
    description=__doc__,
formatter_class=argparse.ArgumentDefaultsHelpFormatter)
    parser.add_argument('project_id', help='Your Cloud
Platform project ID.')
    parser.add_argument('file_name', help='Local file
name')
```

```
args = parser.parse_args()
with open(args.file_name, 'rb') as image:
    result = visionTest(args.project_id, image)
if result == "Upload2GCS":
    result = upload2GCS(args.project_id,
args.file_name)
    print(result)
```

4. Download a sample image (demo-image.jpg) and another image which has a face (name it profile1.jpg):
https://cloud.google.com/vision/docs/images/demo-image.jpg.

5. After installing all the required Python packages, the code can be run as follows:

```
$ python processImage.py <Project ID> demo-image.jpg
Uploaded images does not contains a person's face

$ python processImage.py <Project ID> profile1.jpg
('File uploaded to GCS : ', 'profile1.jpg')
```

Using the Google Cloud Speech API

The Google Speech API uses a powerful machine learning model to convert audio to text. The API recognizes over 110 languages and can process them as a stream or from stored audio files. The Speech API can perform the conversion by three methods—synchronous recognition, asynchronous recognition, and stream recognition.

We'll perform a simple recipe to use the Speech API to convert a recorded message to text using the synchronous recognition method.

Getting ready

The following are the initial setup verification steps for the creation of the network before the recipe can be executed:

1. Create or select a GCP project
2. Enable billing and enable the default APIs (some APIs like BigQuery, storage, monitoring, and few a others are enabled automatically)
3. Enable the Google Cloud Speech API for the project
4. Make sure that the code has access to GCP APIs using the Application Default Credential strategy or direct API keys

How to do it...

First, we'll record the voice which needs to be transcribed in FLAC format. Then, we'll use a Python program to invoke the Speech API and get the transcribed response:

1. Navigate to the `Chapter05/speech-api` folder.

2. If you are on a Linux-based operating system, install the SoX package:

   ```
   $ sudo apt-get install sox
   ```

   Or for CentOS:

   ```
   $ sudo yum install sox
   ```

3. Next, using the `rec` command, we can record the message which needs to be transcribed:

   ```
   $ rec -c 1 -r 16000 record.flac trim 0 3
   ```

   The preceding command will record an audio message for 3 seconds with a sample rate of 16000 Hz.

4. To execute the program in an isolated environment, create a `virtualenv` and install the dependent packages:

   ```
   $ virtualenv ENV
   $ source ENV/bin/activate
   $ pip install -r requirements.txt
   ```

   The following is the contents of the `requirements.txt` file:

   ```
   google-cloud-speech==0.31.1
   ```

5. The following is the program which performs the transcription by invoking the API:

   1. The client libraries are imported:

      ```
      from google.cloud import speech
      from google.cloud.speech import enums
      from google.cloud.speech import types
      ```

   2. The Speech API client is initiated:

      ```
      client = speech.SpeechClient()
      ```

3. The FLAC file recorded in the previous step is mentioned here:

```
file_name = 'record.flac'
```

4. The audio file from the filesystem is loaded into memory, which is pointed out by the `audio` variable:

```
with io.open(file_name, 'rb') as audio_file:
    content = audio_file.read()
    audio = types.RecognitionAudio(content=content)
```

5. The encoding format and the sample rates are configured as follows:

```
config = types.RecognitionConfig(
    encoding='FLAC',
    sample_rate_hertz=16000,
    language_code='en-US')
```

6. The Speech API is invoked and the result is stored in the `response` variable:

```
response = client.recognize(config, audio)
```

6. With the audio file in FLAC format, the API can be invoked and the uttered text is transcribed:

```
(ENV)$ python transcribe.py

Transcript: welcome to Google speech test
```

7. Now, you can try recording different audio FLAC files and invoke the Speech API for transcription.

Using the Cloud IoT Core

Cloud IoT Core is a managed service from the GCP to connect, manage, and send/receive data to IoT devices anywhere in the world. Cloud IoT ensures secure communication with the end devices and seamlessly delivers to a global network of devices.

There are two main components to the IoT Core. The first is the device manager which registers the end devices, which enables us monitor and configure them. The second component is the protocol bridge, which connects the device to the Google Cloud Platform via two protocols—HTTP and MQTT.

To understand the basics, we'll see how to set up a mock IoT device by sending data over HTTP on IoT Core, and how we can read the data which has been sent.

Getting ready

The following are the initial setup verification steps for the creation of the network before the recipe can be executed:

1. Create or select a GCP project
2. Enable billing and enable the default APIs (some APIs like BigQuery, storage, monitoring, and a few others are enabled automatically)
3. Enable the Google Cloud IoT and Cloud Pub/Sub APIs for the project
4. Make sure that the code has access to GCP APIs using the Application Default Credential strategy or direct API keys

How to do it...

In this recipe, we'll see how a hypothetical temperature sensor sends data to IoT Core and how we'll be able to read the telemetry data from the linked Pub/Sub topic:

1. Navigate to the Google Cloud Console's **IoT Core** module and click on **Create device registry**:

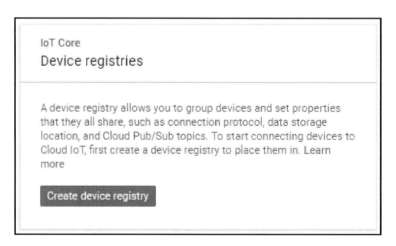

2. Enter the details to create a device registry:

    1. Enter a **Registry ID** and select the **Cloud region** as `us-central1`.

    2. Leave both the protocols selected though we'll send messages via HTTP for this recipe.

    3. For the **Default telemetry topic**, click on **Create a topic**.

    4. Enter a new topic name and click on **CREATE** on the **Create a topic** pop-up screen:

Create a topic

A topic forwards messages from publishers to subscribers.

Name

projects/~~xxxxxxxxxxxx~~/topics/ temperature

CANCEL   CREATE

3. The **Device state topic** is optional. Click on **Create** with all the necessary details filled in:

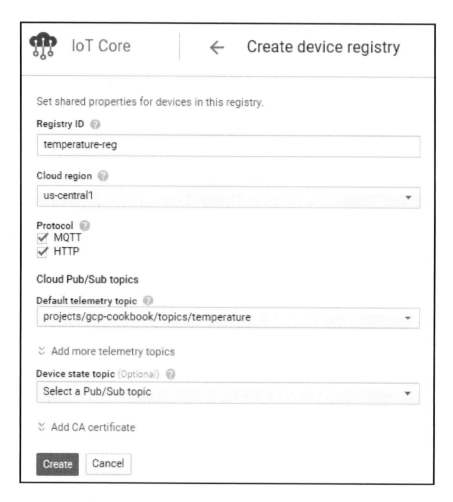

4. Navigate to the Cloud Pub/Sub service and create a pull subscription to the temperature topic which we created in the previous step:

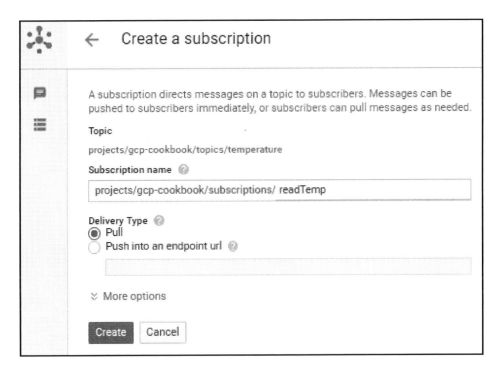

5. Now, let's move on to the development machine which we'll use as a workstation to view the Cloud components and mock it as a IoT temperature device. Let's verify whether we are able to view the subscription we just created from the development machine:

```
$ gcloud pubsub subscriptions list --project=<Project ID>
---
ackDeadlineSeconds: 10
messageRetentionDuration: 604800s
name: projects/<Project ID>/subscriptions/readTemp
pushConfig: {}
topic: projects/<Project ID>/topics/temperature
```

6. Let's create the private and public RS256 keys to be used for the communication between IoT Core and our mocked temperature sensor:

```
openssl genrsa -out tempIoT_private.pem 2048
openssl rsa -in tempIoT_private.pem -pubout -out
tempIoT_public_cert.pem
```

7. The private key will be stored in the IoT device, which in our case, is the mocked development machine. The public key will be stored in the IoT Core device's configuration.

8. Now, let's create the temperate device in Cloud IoT Core. Navigate to the `temperature-reg` registry which we have already created and click on **Add device**.

9. Provide a device name, upload the public certificate generated, and leave the other fields as default:

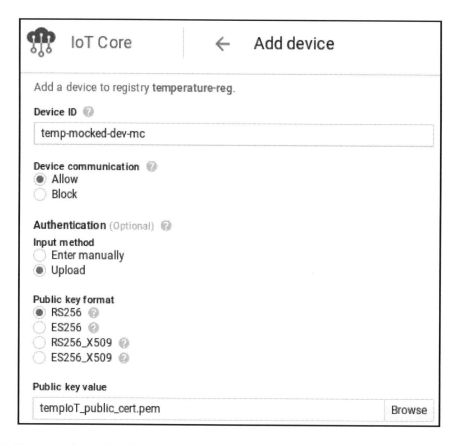

10. Now, we have the device set up in the IoT Core and we get the temperature test to send a message to verify whether it is well received in the Pub/Sub topic.

11. Download the `cloudiot_http_example.py` and `requirements.txt` files from the URL: `https://github.com/GoogleCloudPlatform/python-docs-samples/tree/master/iot/api-client/http_example`.

12. Install the requirements in a `virtualenv` and get the environment ready to run the `cloudiot_http_example.py` program:

```
$ virtualenv ENV
(ENV)$ source ENV/bin/activate
(ENV)$ pip install -r requirements.txt
```

13. Run the Python code to send data to the IoT Core:

```
(ENV)$ python cloudiot-httpexample.py --registry_id=temperature-reg
--project_id=<Project ID> --device_id=temp-mocked-dev-mc --
message_type=event --algorithm=RS256 --
private_key_file=./tempIoT_private.pem
```

14. The `httpexample` code sends sample data, but you can stop the program (*Ctrl + C*) after a few messages have been sent. Use the `gcloud` command to view the message on the Pub/Sub topic:

```
$ gcloud pubsub subscriptions pull --auto-ack readTemp --
project=<Project ID>
```

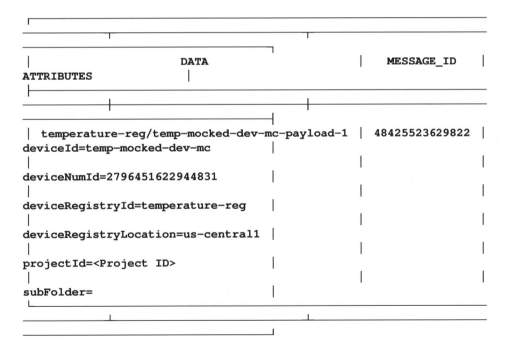

15. Thus, from the development machine, we are able to send data to the IoT Core and read the message from the Pub/Sub topic.

6
Management Tools

In this chapter, we will cover the following recipes:

- Creating alerts on specific events
- Monitoring a web server using Stackdriver monitoring
- Creating tailor-made instances using Deployment Manager
- Error reporting on a Python Flask application
- Viewing application state using Stackdriver Debugger

Introduction

In this chapter, we'll discover a few services in the Stackdriver suite and the deployment manager of **Google Cloud Platform (GCP)**. The Stackdriver suite helps us to watch, debug, and correct the applications running on GCP. It helps us understand the programs running on all the compute platforms of GCP and provides a seamless way to monitor and log their execution. The suite also has diagnostic tools to help developers debug the application in production without introducing any changes for discovering the existing bugs.

We'll perform a few recipes to understand the logging, monitoring, and error reporting capabilities in GCP. We'll be using Python as our language of choice to perform these recipes. Also, we'll use GCP's Deployment Manager to implement the infrastructure-as-code paradigm.

Creating alerts on specific events

Stackdriver Logging is a service provided by GCP to view and analyze log data from instances and applications. With the log events and in conjunction with Stackdriver Monitoring, we can create alerts on log events and notify the concerned users. Stackdriver Monitoring by itself monitors the application components of our applications hosted in GCP and AWS.

Under Stackdriver Logging and Monitoring, let's suppose the administrator of the organization has requested all users of GCP to create instances only in us-west1. The admin has not blocked access via IAM policies to other regions; however, they would like to know if any of the users create any instance outside us-west1. Stackdriver Monitoring provides such a feature to alert the admin in case of a breach of a metric.

Getting ready

The following are the initial setup verification and network creation steps before the recipe can be executed:

1. Create or select a GCP project
2. Enable billing and enable the default APIs (some APIs such as BigQuery, storage, monitoring, and few others are enabled automatically)
3. Make sure the Stackdriver Monitoring and Stackdriver Logging APIs are enabled

How to do it...

To create the automated alerts when a user creates an instance outside our region of choice (us-west1), we'll need to perform two steps. Firstly, we'll have to create custom metric to identify the breach event. Next, we'll create an alerting policy in Stackdriver Monitoring to send us a notification when the conditions of the custom metric are met:

1. Navigate to the **Stackdriver Logging** in the GCP Console.
2. In the resource dropdown, select **GCE VM Instance**, which will show us all logs related to VMs:

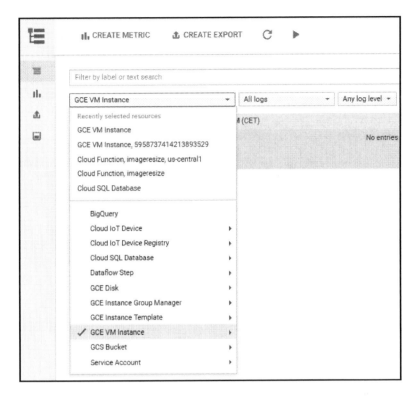

If you don't have any logs for VM creation in your project, create a test VM to generate the activity logs.

3. From the drop-down, select **activity** to filter only the activity-related logs:

4. Now, we can see all the activity related to the VMs in our screen:

5. Expand a log related to an insert event and navigate to the `prototypePayload` section. Then, click on `methodName: "beta.compute.instances.insert"`, which shows you a pop-up menu. In the pop-up menu, select **Show matching entries** to create a new filter for VM create events:

6. By clicking on **Show matching entries**, the filter conditions are created in the top part of the window:

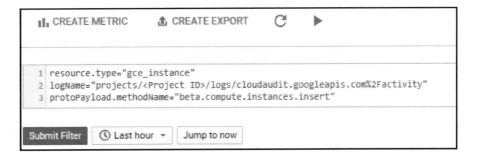

7. This filter gives us all the VM create events. However, we are interested in the VMs created outside the `us-west` region. We'll had a new condition `protoPayload.response.zone` to the existing filter:

```
resource.type="gce_instance"
logName="projects/<Project
ID>/logs/cloudaudit.googleapis.com%2Factivity"
protoPayload.methodName="beta.compute.instances.insert"
NOT resource.labels.zone=("us-west1-c" OR "us-west1-a" OR "us-
west1-b")
```

8. Replace the `Project ID` with your project ID and click on **Submit Filter** to test the syntax and result. To test the filter, create an instance in `us-central1-a` and re-run the filter to view the create activity of the VM in `us-central1-a`:

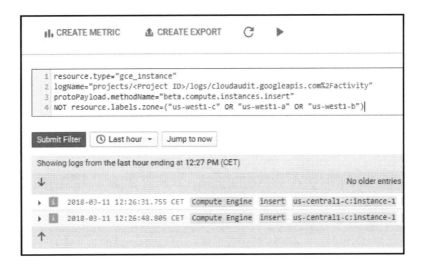

9. Now, click on the **CREATE METRIC** button, give a name to this metric, and create it:

10. Now, you'll see the user-defined metric created in the log-based metrics section. Select **View in Metrics Explorer**, this will take us to the Stackdriver Monitoring application:

11. If the current project is not associated with a Stackdriver account, the monitoring application will request a new account be created or the project be added to an existing account.

12. After the Stackdriver Monitoring account is set up for the project, navigate to the monitoring overview section. Under **Set Altering Policies**, click on **CREATE POLICY**:

13. This takes us to the **Create new alerting policy** page:

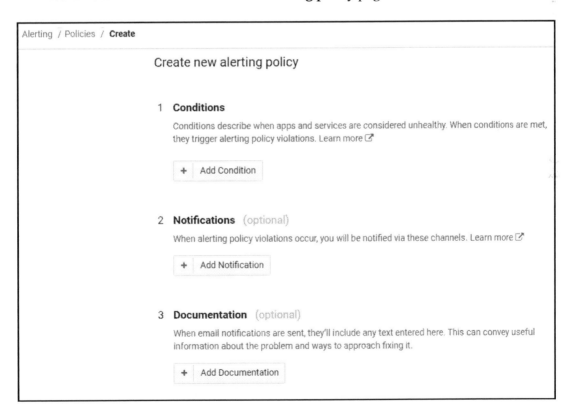

14. Click on **Add Condition** and select the condition type as **Metric Threshold**:

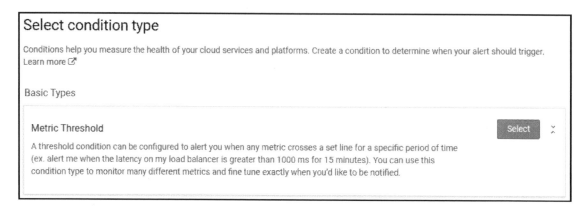

15. In the **Add Metric Threshold Condition** screen, select **Log Metrics** as the resource type. In the **Configuration** section, we'll be able to see our user-defined metric; select our **VM_oustide_US-West** metric and give a threshold of **1**. Then, save the condition:

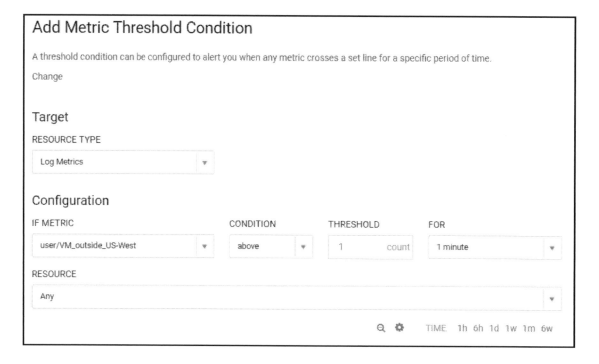

16. Under the **Notifications** section, give an email address to be notified when the metric condition is met:

17. Give a name to the policy and click on **Save Policy**:

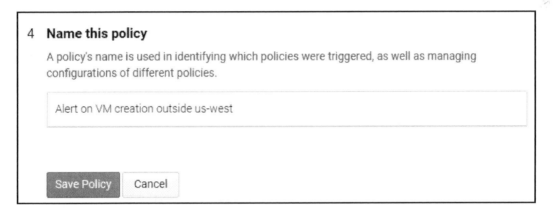

18. Now, if any user creates a VM in any region other than us-west1, the admin will be notified.

Monitoring a webserver using Stackdriver Monitoring

Stackdriver Monitoring is a service of GCP, which tracks the performance of instances and services running on them. Using this service, we can monitor the servers health and hence that of the applications running on them. The service also enables us to create custom metrics and visualize them on dashboards.

To play with the features of Stackdriver Monitoring, we'll setup a new Stackdriver account, install Stackdriver agents on an instance, monitor the instance, create alerting policies, and create metrics dashboard.

Getting ready

The following are the initial setup verification and network creation steps before the recipe can be executed:

1. Create or select a GCP project
2. Enable billing and enable the default APIs (some APIs such as BigQuery, storage, monitoring, and few others are enabled automatically)

How to do it...

In this recipe we'll create an alerting policy to see if the application is up and running. Additionally, we'll also set up an uptime check to see whether the server is up and running:

1. Select your project in the GCP Console and navigate to **Stackdriver | Monitoring**.
2. If monitoring is not setup for your project, you'll see the following screen:

3. You can either create a new Stackdriver account or add the project to an existing account as per your need.

4. Let's create a new Stackdriver account by clicking on **Create Account**:

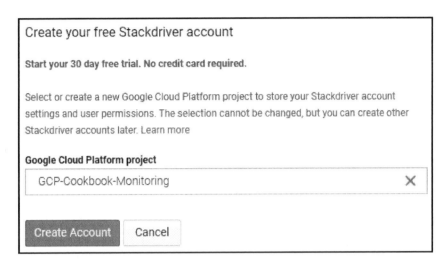

5. In the next step, add the GCP project to be monitored and click on **Continue**:

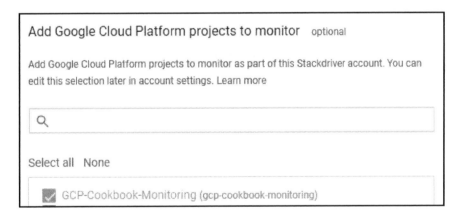

6. You can skip the following AWS setup and continue to the install the Stackdriver agents step. Copy the installation steps to your favorite editor; we'll be using the steps later in the recipe. Click on **Continue** to proceed.

7. Select an interval to receive the Stackdriver reports and continue:

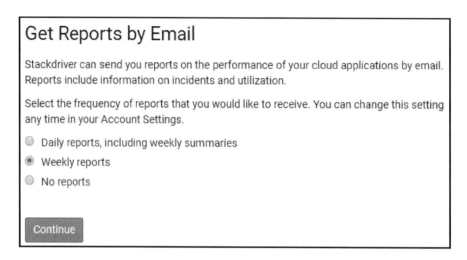

8. Click on **Launch monitoring** to view the Stackdriver Monitoring page:

9. Now, let's create two CentOS 7 and f1-micro instances and monitor them. Make sure you allow HTTP and HTTPS traffic to the machine:

	Name ∧	Zone	Recommendation	Internal IP	External IP	Connect	
☐ ✓	instance-1	us-east1-b		10.142.0.2	35.229.39.6 ↗	SSH ▾	⋮
☐ ✓	instance-2	us-east1-b		10.142.0.3	35.229.81.172 ↗	SSH ▾	⋮

10. SSH into the first instance and install the Stackdriver Monitoring and Stackdriver Logging agents:

```
$ curl -sSO https://repo.stackdriver.com/stack-install.sh
$ sudo bash stack-install.sh --write-gcm
Installing agents for RHEL or CentOS.
warning: /var/cache/yum/x86_64/7/stackdriver/packages/stackdriver-
```

```
agent-5.5.2-379.sdl.el7.centos.x86_64.rpm: Header V3 RSA/SHA1
Signature, key ID 7b190bd2: NOKEY
...
...
Using Cloud Monitoring API
Restarting services
Restarting stackdriver-agent (via systemctl):              [  OK  ]
$ curl -sSO
https://dl.google.com/cloudagents/install-logging-agent.sh
$ sudo bash install-logging-agent.sh
======================================================================
==========
Starting installation of google-fluentd
======================================================================
==========
Installing agents for RHEL or CentOS.
Importing GPG key 0xA7317B0F:
...
...
Starting google-fluentd (via systemctl):                   [  OK  ]
Restarting google-fluentd (via systemctl):                 [  OK  ]
======================================================================
==========
Installation of google-fluentd complete.
...
You can monitor the logging agent's logfile at:
  /var/log/google-fluentd/google-fluentd.log
======================================================================
==========
```

11. Verify that the stackdriver-agent is in running state:

```
$ sudo systemctl status stackdriver-agent
```

12. Install the Apache webserver and start it:

```
$ sudo yum install -y httpd
$ sudo systemctl enable httpd
$ sudo systemctl start httpd
```

13. In your favorite browser, the external IP of the instances should present the **Testing 123..** page of the Apache webserver:

14. Now, let's set up an uptime check for the first instance, `instance-1`. In the Stackdriver Monitoring console, navigate to the **Uptime Checks** menu and click on **Create an Uptime Check**:

> You don't have any uptime checks. Learn more about the uptime monitoring functionality.
>
> Create an Uptime Check

15. Enter a name for the resource type and select **Instance**. Select the instance in the **Applies To** section of the menu. With the other fields as default, click on the **Save** button:

16. You can also create an alerting policy associated with the uptime check:

17. The condition for the alerting policy is filled when you navigate from the uptime check:

18. Update the name of the alerting policy and click on **Save Policy**:

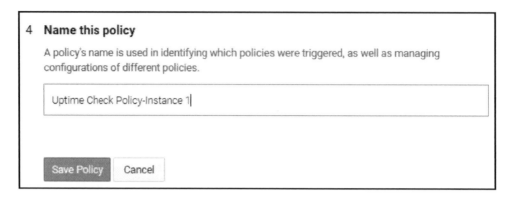

19. The alerting policy is created successfully:

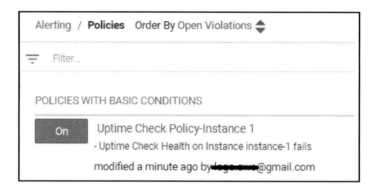

20. Next, let's create a dashboard to view the instance's performance. Navigate to the **Dashboards** menu and click on **Create Dashboard** and give a name to the dashboard.

21. Click on the **ADD CHART** button to view the CPU usage on the GCP instances. Select the resource type as **GCE VM Instance** and **CPU usage** as the metric. Then, click on the **Save** button:

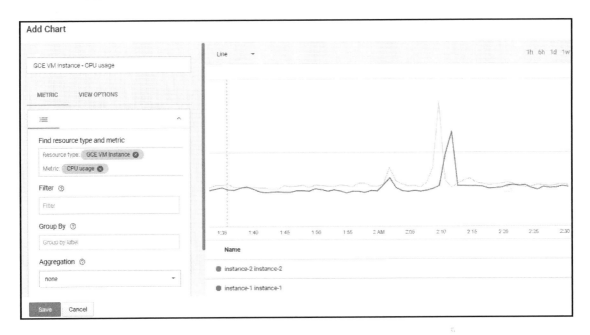

22. You can now view the various monitoring setups. The following screenshot shows the uptime check policy:

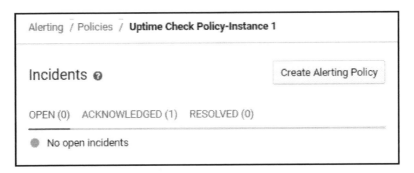

23. The following screenshot shows the **Uptime Check Latency**:

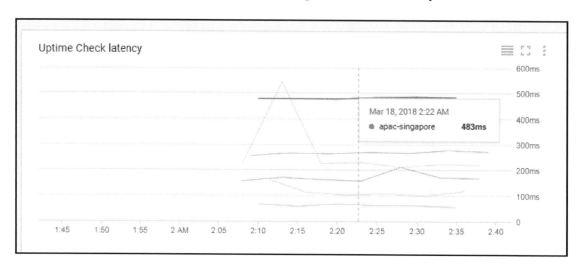

24. The following screenshot shows the dashboard:

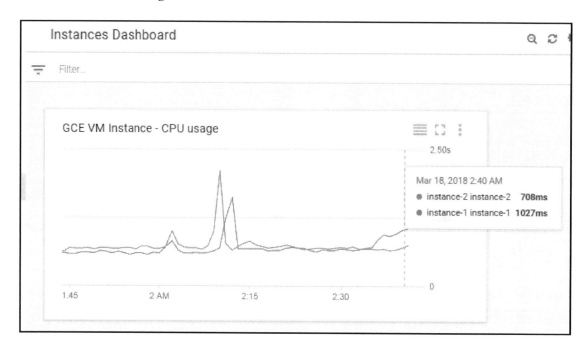

25. You can try stopping the first instance (`instance-1`) and re-verify the monitoring alerts and dashboard.

How it works...

Stackdriver Monitoring uses an open source project, collectd (for more information visit `https://collectd.org/`), to assemble system metrics, application, and custom metrics, which are presented to the user via the Stackdriver Monitoring console.

Creating tailor-made instances using Deployment Manager

GCP provides various options to programmatically create resources needed for an application. The Cloud Deployment Manager provides a repeatable and testable method to specify all the resource needed for an application. The templates can be written in simple YAML files, Jinja templates, and Python templates. The template-driven approach allows us to parameterize and build resources with built-in logic. The templates can be treated as infrastructure as code.

Getting ready

The following are the initial setup verification and network creation steps before the recipe can be executed:

1. Create or select a GCP project
2. Enable billing and enable the default APIs (some APIs such as BigQuery, storage, and monitoring are enabled automatically)

How to do it...

Let's say that organization ABC has a standard practice to keep the application data stored in a non-boot disk and local databases saved in another separate non-boot disk. In this recipe, we'll create an instance with two additional non-boot disks using a simple YAML template and a Jinja template:

1. To create an instance with two additional disk on the GCP Console or `gcloud` command, we'll first have to create the persistent disks separately and then include the created disks in the instance `create` command. Similarly, in the deployment template, we'll first create the two persistent disks.

2. Navigate to the `Chapter06/deploymgr` folder and view the `vm_with_2disks.yaml` file. In the first resource section, we will create two data disks of 10 GB each. You can find the following code in the `vm_with_2disks.yaml` file:

```
resources:
- name: data-disk-1
  type: compute.v1.disk
  properties:
    zone: us-central1-f
    sizeGb: 10
    type: zones/us-central1-f/diskTypes/pd-standard

- name: data-disk-2
  type: compute.v1.disk
  properties:
    zone: us-central1-f
    sizeGb: 11
    type: zones/us-central1-f/diskTypes/pd-standard
```

3. Once the disks are created, we define the parameters required for the instance's creation in the YAML file. The fields defined are very similar to the input parameters of the command `gcloud compute instances create` or the `instances().insert` API call:

```
- type: compute.v1.instance
  name: quickstart-deployment-vm
  properties:
    # The properties of the resource depend on the type of
resource. For a list
    # of properties, see the API reference for the resource.
    zone: us-central1-f
    # Replace [MY_PROJECT] with your project ID
machineType:
```

```
https://www.googleapis.com/compute/v1/projects/upbeat-aura-163616/z
ones/us-central1-f/machineTypes/f1-micro
    disks:
    - deviceName: boot
      type: PERSISTENT
      boot: true
      autoDelete: true
      initializeParams:
        # Replace [FAMILY_NAME] with the image family name.
        # See a full list of image families at
https://cloud.google.com/compute/docs/images#os-compute-support
        sourceImage:
https://www.googleapis.com/compute/v1/projects/debian-cloud/global/
images/family/debian-9
    # Replace [MY_PROJECT] with your project ID
    - deviceName: data-disk-1
      type: PERSISTENT
      source: $(ref.data-disk-1.selfLink)
      boot: false
      autoDelete: true
    - deviceName: data-disk-2
      type: PERSISTENT
      source: $(ref.data-disk-2.selfLink)
      boot: false
      autoDelete: true
    networkInterfaces:
    - network:
https://www.googleapis.com/compute/v1/projects/upbeat-aura-163616/g
lobal/networks/default
      # Access Config required to give the instance a public IP
address
      accessConfigs:
      - name: External NAT
        type: ONE_TO_ONE_NAT
```

4. You can preview the deployment without actually creating the resources. To do so, we'll append the `preview` tag to the `gcloud deployment-manager` command:

```
$ gcloud deployment-manager deployments create quickdeploy --config
vm_with_2disks.yaml --preview
The fingerprint of the deployment is RjND4QB61Xwyb37DY8uMjg==
done.
Create operation
operation-1522016014361-56843f7e0e1a9-809150c6-0c7ddaaf completed
successfully.
NAME                            TYPE            STATE       ERRORS
INTENT
data-disk-1                     compute.v1.disk  IN_PREVIEW  []
CREATE_OR_ACQUIRE
data-disk-2                     compute.v1.disk  IN_PREVIEW  []
CREATE_OR_ACQUIRE
quickstart-deployment-vm  compute.v1.inst  IN_PREVIEW  []
CREATE_OR_ACQUIRE
                                ance
```

5. This clearly shows that the data disks are created and then fed into the VM creation. In the GCP Console, you can navigate to the **Deployment Manager** and go to **Deployments**:

6. Expanding on the deployment reveals the details of the resources created and their parameters:

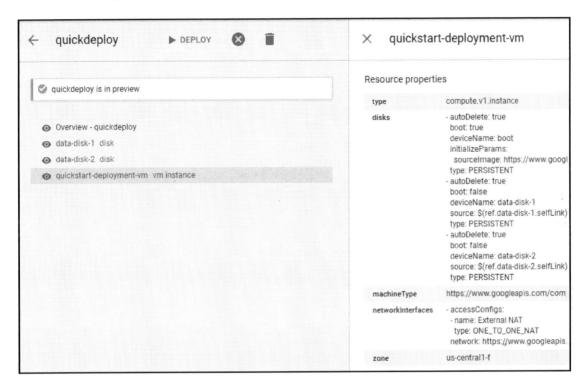

7. You can complete the deployment by clicking on the **DEPLOY** button on the GCP Console or by using the `gcloud` command:

```
gcloud deployment-manager deployments update quickdeploy
The fingerprint of the deployment is jtRRK0b6bMHn0hfiqfO82A==
done.
Update operation operation-1522017772469-5684460ab7b09-
fc5648e4-0bd804f0 completed successfully.
NAME                       TYPE                  STATE       ERRORS
INTENT
data-disk-1                compute.v1.disk       COMPLETED   []
data-disk-2                compute.v1.disk       COMPLETED   []
quickstart-deployment-vm   compute.v1.instance   COMPLETED   []
```

8. The deployment has successfully completed:

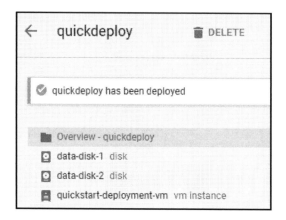

9. You can also find the instance's details in the VM instances console:

10. We'll also try to deploy the same machine using the Jinja template. One of the advantages of the Jinja template is the ability to have an expressive language for the template. We have taken the `vm_with_disks` sample from the GCP GitHub repository. Open the `vm_with_disks.jinja` and `vm_with_disks.yaml` files.

11. To create the two disks, you find a `for` loop in the Jinja template to iterate over the two input disk definitions from the YAML file. You can also note that the Jinja templates read the project ID from the default project set in the local configuration. You can find the following code in the `vm_with_disks.jinja` file:

```
resources:

{% for diskObj in properties["disks"] %}
- name: {{ diskName(diskObj) }}
  type: compute.v1.disk
  properties:
    zone: {{ properties["zone"] }}
    sizeGb: {{ diskObj["sizeGb"] }}
    type: https://www.googleapis.com/compute/v1/projects/{{
env["project"] }}/zones/{{ properties["zone"] }}/diskTypes/{{
diskObj["diskType"] }}
{% endfor %}
```

12. You can now deploy the same configuration using the Jinja template:

```
$ gcloud deployment-manager deployments create vm2disk-deploy --
config vm_with_disks.yaml
The fingerprint of the deployment is msfhBn9oY1OWS1DgjilEeQ==
done.
Create operation operation-1522018448369-5684488f4e569-4b9d9b8a-
a1ddb662 completed successfully.
NAME                          TYPE                 STATE        ERRORS
INTENT
vm2disk-deploy-disk-backup    compute.v1.disk      COMPLETED    []
vm2disk-deploy-disk-cache     compute.v1.disk      COMPLETED    []
vm2disk-deploy-vm             compute.v1.instance  COMPLETED    []
```

13. You can delete the deployments to kill the machines created by the deployment:

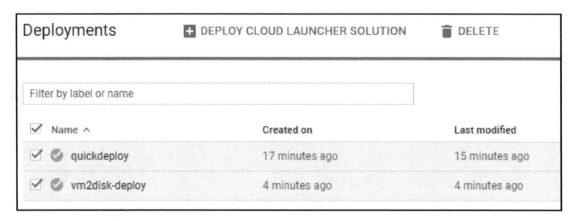

Error Reporting on a Python Flask application

Stackdriver Error Reporting is a service to capture and display the errors occurring in the compute services of GCP—App Engine, Cloud Functions, and Compute Engine. The applications developed in Go, Java, .NET, Node.js, Python, and Ruby can use the Error Reporting. Once the Error Reporting is set up, the service captures the errors automatically and in real-time. The captured errors can be viewed in the GCP web console and alerts can be set for notification.

Getting ready

The following are the initial setup verification and network creation steps before the recipe can be executed:

1. Create or select a GCP project
2. Enable billing and enable the default APIs (some APIs such as BigQuery, storage, monitoring, and few others are enabled automatically)
3. Enable the Stackdriver Error Reporting API

How to do it...

In this recipe, we'll create a Linux instance and run a simple Flask application. In the web application, we'll write code to capture an error and send it to Stackdriver Error Reporting:

1. Let's first create an instance to host our Flask application. Note that the access scope allows full access to all Cloud APIs:

```
$ gcloud compute instances create flask-instance --image=debian-9-
stretch-v20180307 --image-project "debian-cloud" --machine-type=f1-
micro --scopes cloud-platform --zone us-east1-c --tags flask-server
--project <Project ID>
```

2. Next, we'll open the firewall for this instance (network tag: flask-server) on port 5000:

```
$ gcloud compute firewall-rules create default-allow-http-5000 --
allow tcp:5000 --source-ranges 0.0.0.0/0 --target-tags flask-server
--description "Allow port 5000 access to flask-server" --project
<Project ID>
```

3. Before we SSH into the instance and create the web app, we'll make a small modification to the default service account of the compute engine which would have been used when the instance was created. In the GCP console, navigate to the **IAM & Admin | IAM**:

4. In the filter, type Compute Engine default service account:

5. Now, we'll add the **Errors Writer** role to the service account:

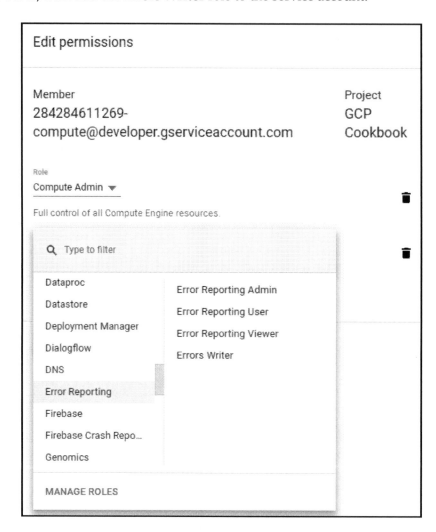

6. Now, the permissions screen will show the new role added to the service account:

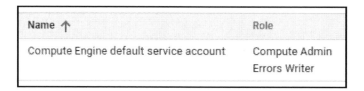

7. Let's head back to the Compute Engine console and SSH into the Flask instance created. Verify that Python is installed and install PIP on the VM:

```
$ python --version
$ sudo apt-get install python-pip -y
```

8. We'll install the `Flask` package and the `google-cloud-error-reporting` package on the machine:

```
$ pip install Flask
$ pip install google-cloud-error-reporting --upgrade
```

9. Create a `hello.py` file and move the contents of the `Chapter06/error-reporting/hello.py` to the server. The following simple code instantiates a Flask server on port `5000`. On the `/error` route, an error is raised manually to simulate an error condition. The raised error is sent to the Error Reporting API. You can see the following code in the `hello.py` file:

```
# Sample code to demonstrate GCP Error Reporting
from flask import Flask
app = Flask(__name__)
#
https://github.com/GoogleCloudPlatform/python-docs-samples/blob/mas
ter/error_reporting/api/report_exception.py

def simulate_error():
    from google.cloud import error_reporting
    client = error_reporting.Client()
    try:
        # simulate calling a method that's not defined
        raise NameError
    except Exception:
        client.report_exception()

def report_manual_error():
    from google.cloud import error_reporting
    client = error_reporting.Client()
    client.report("An error has occurred.")

@app.route('/')
def hello_world():
    return 'Hello World!'
@app.route('/error')

def error_reporting():
    simulate_error()
```

```
        report_manual_error()

if __name__ == '__main__':
    app.run(host='0.0.0.0')
```

10. Run the sample Flask as follows:

```
$ python hello.py
* Running on http://0.0.0.0:5000/ (Press CTRL+C to quit)
```

11. On your favorite browser, point to the external IP of the instance on port 5000. The following are the details of the instance:

12. The following is the application on the browser:

13. Now, to generate the error, navigate to the URL /error:

14. The Flask logs show the error generated:

```
62.129.12.26 - - [20/Mar/2018 00:15:51] "GET / HTTP/1.1" 200 -
[2018-03-20 00:16:05,540] ERROR in app: Exception on /error [GET]
Traceback (most recent call last):
  File "/home/xxxx/.local/lib/python2.7/site-
packages/flask/app.py", line 1982, in wsgi_app
    response = self.full_dispatch_request()
  File "/home/xxxx/.local/lib/python2.7/site-
packages/flask/app.py", line 1615, in full_dispatch_request
    return self.finalize_request(rv)
  File "/home/xxxx/.local/lib/python2.7/site-
```

```
packages/flask/app.py", line 1630, in finalize_request
    response = self.make_response(rv)
  File "/home/xxxx/.local/lib/python2.7/site-
packages/flask/app.py", line 1725, in make_response
    raise ValueError('View function did not return a response')
ValueError: View function did not return a response
62.129.12.26 - - [20/Mar/2018 00:16:05] "GET /error HTTP/1.1" 500 -
```

15. On the GCP Console, navigate to the **Error Reporting** under the **Stackdriver** section to view the error:

If you see **PermissionDenied: 403** in the Flask logs, make sure you do the following:

- The service account used by the instance has been granted the Error Reporting Write role.
- The Stackdriver Error Reporting API is enabled to the project.

Viewing application state using Stackdriver Debugger

Stackdriver Debugger is a feature that lets us understand the state of the application in order to help the developer debug the application in production and in its running state. The debugger can be set up by adding additional code to the program, or it is enabled by default in some computing platforms such as the App Engine. Once the debugger is setup, the state of application variables can be viewed as debug snapshots and new logging steps can be enabled by injecting logging statements using debug logpoints.

Getting ready

The following are the initial setup verifications and network creation before the recipe can be executed:

1. Create or select a GCP Project
2. Enable billing and enable the default APIs (some APIs such as BigQuery, storage, monitoring and few others are enabled automatically)
3. Enable the Stackdriver Error Debugger API
4. Verify if the Cloud Source Repositories API is enabled

How to do it...

In this recipe, we'll run a Flask application, similar to the previous recipe, to demonstrate the debugging facility of the Stackdriver debugger. In addition to running it, the debugger should have access to the code base; in our example we'll upload the code to Google Cloud Repositories:

1. Create the Flask VM similar to the previous recipe (*step 1* and *step 2*) or you can re-use the machine created.
2. SSH into the VM and make sure Python and PIP are installed.
3. Install Git using the following command:

```
$ sudo apt-get update
$ sudo apt-get install git
```

4. Let's move out of the VM, launch a Google Cloud Shell, and create a Google source code repository. If you want to run the gcloud command to create the repository from the VM, the service account attached to the VM should have appropriate privileges:

```
$ gcloud source repos create flaskApp --project gcp-cookbook
```

5. Now, back to the SSH window of the VM, let's clone the `flaskApp`. Move the contents of `Chapter06/debugger` to the `flaskApp` folder and initialize a new Git repository in the folder:

```
$ gcloud source repos clone flaskApp
#FYA: ... Move the helloDebug.py and requirements.txt from the
Chapter06/debugger folder ...
~/flaskApp$ ls
helloDebug.py requirements.txt
```

6. Install the required Python packages and run the Flask application to verify the web app location runs fine:

```
$ pip install -r requirements.txt
$ python helloDebug.py
 * Running on http://0.0.0.0:5000/ (Press CTRL+C to quit)
62.129.12.26 - - [22/Mar/2018 10:31:13] "GET / HTTP/1.1" 200 -
62.129.12.26 - - [22/Mar/2018 10:31:13] "GET /favicon.ico HTTP/1.1"
404 -
```

7. The web page is available on port `5000`. Use you favorite browser to view the web application:

8. Add both the files to Git and commit our setup:

```
$ git add helloDebug.py requirements.txt
$ git commit -m 'Files set up for debugger'
[master (root-commit) 1fffdd9] Files set up for debugger
 2 files changed, 23 insertions(+)
 create mode 100644 helloDebug.py
 create mode 100644 requirements.txt
```

9. Now, let's push the code to Google source repositories:

```
$ git push origin master
Counting objects: 4, done.
Compressing objects: 100% (3/3), done.
Writing objects: 100% (4/4), 688 bytes | 0 bytes/s, done.
Total 4 (delta 0), reused 0 (delta 0)
To https://source.developers.google.com/p/gcp-cookbook/r/flaskApp
 * [new branch]        master -> master
```

10. We can invoke the Google Cloud debugger by making code modifications to the application or by invoking the agent on the VM. Let's now install the Google Cloud debugger agent on the machine:

```
$ pip install google-python-cloud-debugger
```

11. We'll now run the debugger agent as a module:

```
$ python -m googleclouddebugger --module=FlaskApp --version=v1 --
helloDebug.py
 * Running on http://0.0.0.0:5000/ (Press CTRL+C to quit)
I0322 11:33:06.480788  1278 gcp_hub_client.py:336] Debuggee
registered successfully, ID: gcp:284284611269:ff2cdedf989c231a
```

12. Note that the service account has the **Stackdriver Debugger Agent** role attached to it:

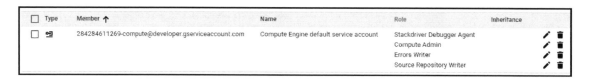

	Type	Member ↑	Name	Role	Inheritance	
☐	☐	284284611269-compute@developer.gserviceaccount.com	Compute Engine default service account	Stackdriver Debugger Agent		✎ 🗑
				Compute Admin		✎ 🗑
				Errors Writer		✎ 🗑
				Source Repository Writer		✎ 🗑

13. You can trigger the `http://<External IP Address>:5000/add/1,2,2` path of the website to get the sum of the numbers passed:

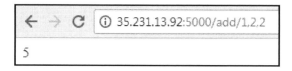

14. In the GCP console, navigate to the debug application under Stackdriver. For the debugger to work, it needs to know about the application source code. Click on the **Select source** button under the **Cloud Source Repositories**:

15. Select our **flaskApp** repository and click on **SELECT SOURCE**:

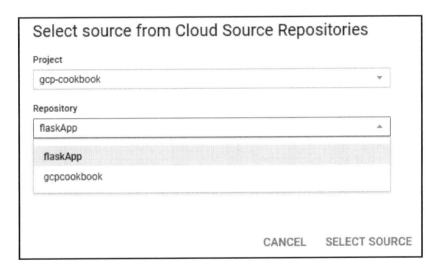

16. The debugger window will warn us of the service account's insufficient access. Click on the **Fix** button to resolve the access issue. This adds the project editor access to the service account. Adding this at the get go might resolve most of the access issues (HTTP 403 errors) that you might receive in various stages:

17. Mark a statement to watch on the debugger:

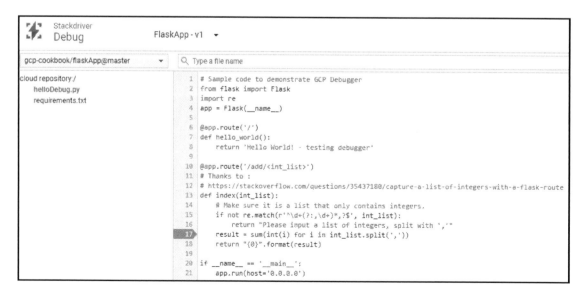

18. And now, launch the application URL `http://<External IP Address>:5000/add/1,2,2` in the browser and watch the result of the statement in the debugger window:

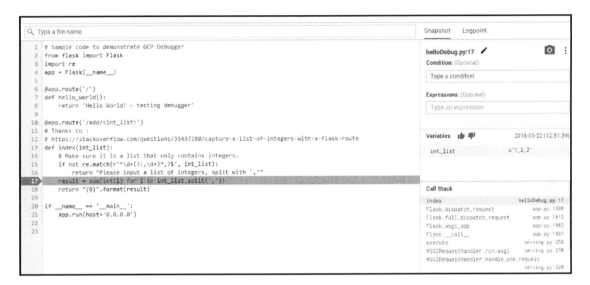

19. This allows us to debug an application in production without impacting the user's experience.

7
Best Practices

In this chapter, we will cover:

- Creating a custom VM using Terraform
- Monitoring a GCP account using Security Monkey
- Creating instance backups
- Simulating VM migration
- Creating a Golden Image using Packer

Introduction

In this chapter, we'll get a taste of some of the best practices and solutions that are performed at an enterprise level. Enterprises demand stricter policies and processes to allow the ability for multiple stakeholders to work in a robust environment. When a developer creates an instance, not a lot of thought is put into the ports being opened, password policies, and infrastructure policies. On the other hand, at an enterprise level, for each component of the infrastructure, a specific person or role is defined to ensure a smooth operation.

This chapter covers a few topics on how instances are managed, migration of instances, and tools that ensure and enable industry-grade operations.

Creating a custom VM using Terraform

Terraform is a powerful tool used for defining infrastructure as code on various platforms. Two of the biggest advantages of Terraform are its simple templating language (**HashiCorp Configuration Language**, also known as **HCL**) and its state maintenance. Terraform's role of provisioning plays well with other configuration management tools. The configurations given to Terraform are converted into API calls to perform the provisioning. Also, when a change is made to the desired state, for example, the count of instances is updated from two to three, Terraform keeps track of the state and launches the creation of one new instance.

In this recipe, similar to the tailor-made VM we created using the Deployment Manager in the previous chapter, we will create a simple VM with two additional disks using Terraform.

Getting ready

The following are the initial setup verification steps before the recipe can be executed:

1. Create or select a GCP project
2. Enable billing and enable the default APIs (some APIs such as BigQuery, storage, monitoring, and a few others are enabled automatically)
3. Verify that GOOGLE_APPLICATION_CREDENTIALS is properly set
4. Install Terraform from the official website (https://www.terraform.io/intro/getting-started/install.html)

How to do it...

After the successful installation of Terraform on your machine, we'll build the Terraform configuration setup step by step:

1. Set up the environment variables and the Google Cloud provider block
2. Create the two additional compute disks
3. Create the VM with two additional disks

Let's look into these steps in detail:

1. The code for this recipe can be found in the `Chapter07/terraform` file. The first part of configuring Terraform is setting up the Google Cloud provider, which is as follows. Save the configuration to a file, `example.tf`:

```
// Configure the Google Cloud provider
provider "google" {
  project     = "<Project ID>"
  region      = "us-central1"
}
```

2. To execute the configuration, the provider needs to possess proper credentials. Credentials can be explicitly given in the provider section using the credentials key, `credentials = "${file("account.json")}"`. In our case, if `GOOGLE_APPLICATION_CREDENTIALS` is properly set, Terraform will use the path that has been stored.

3. Now, let's execute the first `init` command to initialize the local settings and data:

```
$ terraform init

Initializing provider plugins...
- Checking for available provider plugins on
https://releases.hashicorp.com...
- Downloading plugin for provider "google" (1.8.0)...

...

* provider.google: version = "~> 1.8"

Terraform has been successfully initialized!

You may now begin working with Terraform. Try running "terraform
plan" to see
...
```

4. Next, we'll create the two disks that are going to be used by the instance. The two disks are of different types, and they have different names. To hold the disk type and disk name, we'll create local variables. Then, in the `resource` block, we will invoke the resource type, `google_compute_disk`, and give it a name, `AddlnDisks`. Within the disk block, the configuration for the Compute Engine disks is given. To create two disks, we'll use Terraform's meta-parameter, `count`, which is part of most resource types:

```
variable "diskType" {
  description = "Disk types"
  type = "list"
  default = ["pd-standard", "pd-ssd"]
}

variable "diskName" {
  description = "Disk Name"
  type = "list"
  default = ["backup", "cache"]
}

//
https://www.terraform.io/docs/providers/google/r/compute_disk.h
tml#

resource "google_compute_disk" "AddlnDisks" {
  count = 2
  name  = "${element(var.diskName, count.index)}"
  type  = "${element(var.diskType, count.index)}"
  zone  = "us-central1-a"
  size = 10
  labels {
    environment = "dev"
  }
}
```

5. You can now run Terraform plan to view the execution plan for the two disks:

```
$ terraform plan
. . .
Terraform will perform the following actions:

  + google_compute_disk.AddlnDisks[0]
      id:                       <computed>
      disk_encryption_key_sha256: <computed>
      label_fingerprint:        <computed>
      labels.%:                 "1"
```

```
        labels.environment:       "dev"
        name:                     "backup"
        project:                  <computed>
        self_link:                <computed>
        size:                     "10"
        type:                     "pd-standard"
        users.#:                  <computed>
        zone:                     "us-central1-a"

+ google_compute_disk.AddlnDisks[1]
        id:                          <computed>
        disk_encryption_key_sha256:  <computed>
        label_fingerprint:           <computed>
        labels.%:                    "1"
        labels.environment:          "dev"
        name:                        "cache"
        project:                     <computed>
        self_link:                   <computed>
        size:                        "10"
        type:                        "pd-ssd"
        users.#:                     <computed>
        zone:                        "us-central1-a"


Plan: 2 to add, 0 to change, 0 to destroy.
```

6. In the following part, we'll create the instance resource and attach the two disks. Most of the arguments for the compute instance resource type are self-explanatory; the details of the required and optional arguments can be found in Terraform's documentation. The `attached_disk` section contains the data from the `google_compute_disk` section. We will also set an explicit dependency for the creation of the instance only after the disks are created using the `depends_on` argument, though it is not required because Terraform understands an implicit dependency between the disks and the instance:

```
resource "google_compute_instance" "instance1" {
  name          = "vm-with-disks"
  machine_type  = "f1-micro"
  zone          = "us-central1-a"

  tags = ["foo", "bar"]

  boot_disk {
    initialize_params {
      image = "debian-cloud/debian-8"
    }
```

```
        }

    attached_disk {
            source      =
"${element(google_compute_disk.AddlnDisks.*.self_link, 1)}"
            device_name =
"${element(google_compute_disk.AddlnDisks.*.name, 1)}"
        }
    attached_disk {
            source      =
"${element(google_compute_disk.AddlnDisks.*.self_link, 2)}"
            device_name =
"${element(google_compute_disk.AddlnDisks.*.name, 2)}"
        }

    network_interface {
        network = "default"

        access_config {
            // Ephemeral IP
        }
    }

    metadata {
        foo = "bar"
    }

    metadata_startup_script = "echo hi > /test.txt"

    service_account {
        scopes = ["userinfo-email", "compute-ro", "storage-ro"]
    }

    depends_on = ["google_compute_disk.default"]
}

output "instance_id" {
    value = "${google_compute_instance.default.self_link}"
}
```

7. You can run Terraform plan to view the creation of these three resources:

```
$ terraform plan
....
  + google_compute_instance.instance1
        id:
<computed>
        attached_disk.#:                                        "2"
```

```
        attached_disk.0.device_name:                    "cache"
        attached_disk.0.disk_encryption_key_sha256:
<computed>
        attached_disk.0.mode:
"READ_WRITE"
....
        tags_fingerprint:
<computed>
        zone:                                           "us-
central1-a"

Plan: 3 to add, 0 to change, 0 to destroy.
```

8. Finally, with the configuration complete, we can now execute the `terraform apply` command in order to execute the creation of the resources in the GCP:

```
$ terraform apply

Terraform will perform the following actions:

  + google_compute_disk.AddlnDisks[0]
      id:
<computed>
...
  + google_compute_disk.AddlnDisks[1]
      id:
<computed>
...
  + google_compute_instance.instance1
      id:
<computed>
...
      attached_disk.0.source:
"${element(google_compute_disk.AddlnDisks.*.self_link, 1)}"
...
      attached_disk.1.source:
"${element(google_compute_disk.AddlnDisks.*.self_link, 2)}"
      boot_disk.#:                                      "1"
...
      zone:                                             "us-
central1-a"


Plan: 3 to add, 0 to change, 0 to destroy.

Do you want to perform these actions?
  Terraform will perform the actions described above.
```

```
Only 'yes' will be accepted to approve.

Enter a value: yes

google_compute_disk.AddlnDisks[0]: Creating...
  disk_encryption_key_sha256: "" => "<computed>"
...
google_compute_disk.AddlnDisks.1: Still creating... (10s elapsed)
google_compute_disk.AddlnDisks.0: Still creating... (10s elapsed)
google_compute_disk.AddlnDisks[0]: Creation complete after 12s (ID:
backup)
google_compute_disk.AddlnDisks[1]: Creation complete after 13s (ID:
cache)
google_compute_instance.instance1: Creating...
  attached_disk.#:                                "" => "2"
  attached_disk.0.device_name:                    "" =>
"cache"
...
  zone:                                           "" => "us-
central1-a"
google_compute_instance.instance1: Still creating... (10s elapsed)
google_compute_instance.instance1: Creation complete after 13s (ID:
vm-with-disks)

Apply complete! Resources: 3 added, 0 changed, 0 destroyed.

Outputs:

instance_id =
https://www.googleapis.com/compute/v1/projects/upbeat-aura-163616/z
ones/us-central1-a/instances/vm-with-disks
```

9. Thus, using Terraform, we can execute a repeatable infrastructure and treat infrastructure-as-code at an enterprise scale.

10. To clean up the created resources, you can execute the `terraform destroy` command:

```
$ terraform destroy
...
Terraform will perform the following actions:

  - google_compute_disk.AddlnDisks[0]
  - google_compute_disk.AddlnDisks[1]
  - google_compute_instance.instance1

Plan: 0 to add, 0 to change, 3 to destroy.
```

```
Do you really want to destroy?
  Terraform will destroy all your managed infrastructure, as shown
above.
  There is no undo. Only 'yes' will be accepted to confirm.

  Enter a value: yes

google_compute_instance.instance1: Destroying... (ID: vm-with-
disks)
google_compute_instance.instance1: Still destroying... (ID: vm-
with-disks, 40s elapsed)
google_compute_instance.instance1: Destruction complete after 46s
google_compute_disk.AddlnDisks[1]: Destroying... (ID: cache)
google_compute_disk.AddlnDisks[0]: Destroying... (ID: backup)
google_compute_disk.AddlnDisks.0: Still destroying... (ID: backup,
10s elapsed)
google_compute_disk.AddlnDisks.1: Still destroying... (ID: cache,
10s elapsed)
google_compute_disk.AddlnDisks[1]: Destruction complete after 12s
google_compute_disk.AddlnDisks[0]: Destruction complete after 12s

Destroy complete! Resources: 3 destroyed.
```

Monitoring a GCP account using Security Monkey

Monitoring the data center is an important job in the day-to-day operations of DC maintenance. Different parameters are monitored—usage of resources, idle time, software updates, performance logs, security logs, and so on. This helps administrators take preventive and corrective actions against events. Security Monkey is an open source monitoring tool developed initially by the team at Netflix to monitor their AWS infrastructure. Currently a lot of development is underway to support more and more GCP services.

In this recipe, we'll use Security Monkey on our GCP infrastructure and look at how it can be used for monitoring at an organization level.

Getting ready

The following are the initial setup verification steps before the recipe can be executed:

1. Create or select a GCP project
2. Enable billing and enable the default APIs (some APIs like BigQuery, storage, monitoring, and a few others are enabled automatically)
3. Enable the Google **Identity and Access Management (IAM)** API

How to do it...

To perform this recipe, we'll install Security Monkey and the database needed for the application: a single Ubuntu instance. For most of this recipe, we'll follow the guidelines from Security Monkey's GitHub documentation:

1. First, we'll create a service account called `securitymonkey` and provide it with the necessary access. Create a JSON access key for the service account and save it in a safe location:

2. We'll add the **Viewer** and **Security Reviewer** roles to the service account we just created:

3. We'll now create an Ubuntu 16.04 LTS machine with the created `securitymonkey` service account:

```
$ gcloud compute --project=<Project ID> instances create
securitymonkey --zone=us-central1-c --machine-type=n1-standard-1 --
service-account=securitymonkey@<Project ID>.iam.gserviceaccount.com
--scopes=https://www.googleapis.com/auth/cloud-platform --
tags=https-server --image=ubuntu-1604-xenial-v20180323 --image-
project=ubuntu-os-cloud --boot-disk-size=10GB --boot-disk-type=pd-
standard --boot-disk-device-name=securitymonkey
```

4. SSH into the instance and install the prerequisite software:

```
$ sudo apt-get update
$ sudo apt-get -y install python-pip python-dev python-psycopg2
postgresql postgresql-contrib libpq-dev nginx supervisor git
libffi-dev gcc python-virtualenv redis-server
```

5. Then, we'll install Postgres locally, on the machine:

```
$ sudo apt-get install postgresql postgresql-contrib
$ sudo -u postgres psql
postgres=# CREATE DATABASE "secmonkey";
CREATE DATABASE
postgres=# CREATE ROLE "securitymonkeyuser" LOGIN PASSWORD
'securitymonkeypassword';
CREATE ROLE
postgres=# CREATE SCHEMA secmonkey;
CREATE SCHEMA
postgres=# GRANT Usage, Create ON SCHEMA "secmonkey" TO
"securitymonkeyuser";
GRANT
postgres=# set timezone TO 'GMT';
SET
postgres=# select now();
postgres=# \q
```

6. Next, we'll create the logging folders that are required by the tool:

```
sudo mkdir /var/log/security_monkey
sudo mkdir /var/www
sudo chown -R `whoami`:www-data /var/log/security_monkey/
sudo chown www-data /var/www
```

7. Following the steps in the Security Monkey GitHub docs, we'll clone the `security_monkey` master branch and complete the setup:

```
$ cd /usr/local/src
$ sudo git clone --depth 1 --branch develop
https://github.com/Netflix/security_monkey.git
$ sudo chown -R `whoami`:www-data /usr/local/src/security_monkey
$ cd security_monkey
$ export LC_ALL="en_US.UTF-8"
$ export LC_CTYPE="en_US.UTF-8"
$ virtualenv venv
$ source venv/bin/activate
$ pip install --upgrade setuptools
$ pip install --upgrade pip
$ pip install --upgrade urllib3[secure]
$ pip install google-compute-engine
$ pip install cloudaux\[gcp\]
$ python setup.py develop
```

8. To create the database tables, we'll use the `monkey` command under the virtual environment:

```
(venv) :/usr/local/src/security_monkey$ monkey db upgrade
. . . .
[ ] Setting primary key values for the 'association' table...
[+] Completed setting primary key values for 'association'
[ ] Setting primary key values for the 'roles_users' table...
[+] Completed setting primary key values for 'roles_users' [+]
Done!
```

9. Next, we'll add our GCP account to the Security Monkey setup:

```
(venv) :/usr/local/src/security_monkey$ monkey add_account_gcp -n
test-env --id <GCP Project ID>
```

10. We'll also create our first user for the tool so that it can be used in the web UI:

```
$ monkey create_user "name@example.com" "Admin"
> Password:
> Confirm Password:
```

11. Next, we'll create a self-signed SSL certificate that will be used by the Security Monkey web application. We'll use Ubuntu's guide for self-signed SSL creation for this step:

```
(venv) :/usr/local/src/security_monkey$ cd ~
(venv) :~$ openssl genrsa -des3 -out server.key 2048
Generating RSA private key, 2048 bit long modulus
.......................................+++
...........................+++
e is 65537 (0x10001)
Enter pass phrase for server.key:
Verifying - Enter pass phrase for server.key:
(venv) :~$ openssl rsa -in server.key -out server.key.insecure
Enter pass phrase for server.key:
writing RSA key
(venv) :~$ mv server.key server.key.secure
(venv) :~$ mv server.key.insecure server.key
(venv) :~$ openssl req -new -key server.key -out server.csr
<... Enter details ....>
(venv) :~$ openssl x509 -req -days 365 -in server.csr -signkey
server.key -out server.crt
Signature ok
...
Getting Private key
(venv) :~$ sudo cp server.crt /etc/ssl/certs
(venv) :~$ sudo cp server.key /etc/ssl/private
```

12. Next, let's download the stable version of the web UI in the `security_monkey` folder. The latest release of the UI is at: `https://github.com/Netflix/security_monkey/releases/latest`:

```
$ cd /usr/local/src/security_monkey/security_monkey
$ wget
https://github.com/Netflix/security_monkey/releases/download/v1.0.0
/static.tar.gz
$ tar -xvzf static.tar.gz
$ sudo chgrp -R www-data /usr/local/src/security_monkey
```

13. After the UI code is downloaded, manually start the Security Monkey application. Make sure you run the application under the Python virtual environment:

```
$ cd /usr/local/src/security_monkey/security_monkey
$ (venv) :/usr/local/src/security_monkey/security_monkey$ monkey
run_api_server
```

14. To launch the web UI, use the external IP of the instance in your web browser and log in with the user we have already created:

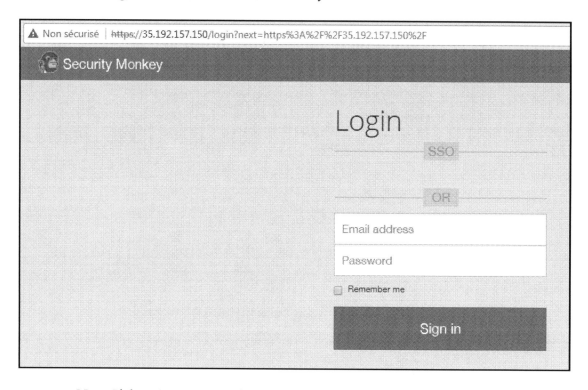

Note: If there is a security alert on the external IP, do accept the security exception temporarily.

15. After you log in to the application, navigate to **Settings | Accounts** and click on the account. Upload the JSON credentials file to the instance and then provide the complete path location. Also, make sure to click the **Active** checkbox to enable the account:

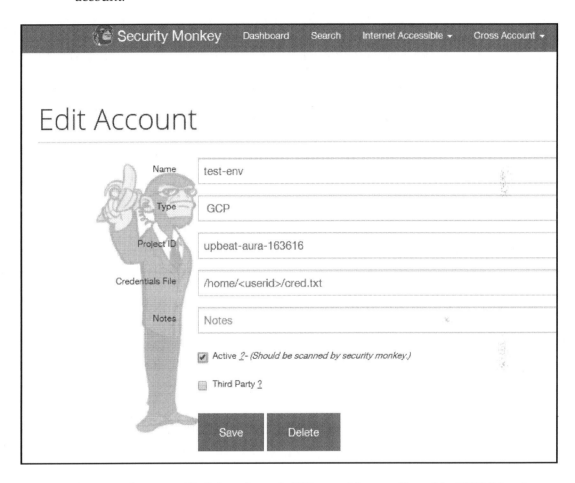

16. Once we have verified that the web UI is working, we'll enable NGINX and supervisor to `autostart` the application:

```
$ sudo chgrp -R www-data /var/log/security_monkey
$ sudo cp
/usr/local/src/security_monkey/supervisor/security_monkey_ui.conf
/etc/supervisor/conf.d/security_monkey_ui.conf
$ sudo systemctl enable nginx
$ sudo systemctl enable supervisor
```

```
$ sudo systemctl start nginx
$ sudo systemctl start supervisor
$ sudo supervisorctl status
```

17. As a following step, we'll provide the supervisor configuration:

```
$ sudo chgrp -R www-data /var/log/security_monkey
$ sudo cp
/usr/local/src/security_monkey/supervisor/security_monkey_scheduler
.conf /etc/supervisor/conf.d/security_monkey_scheduler.conf
$ sudo systemctl enable supervisor
$ sudo systemctl start supervisor
$ sudo supervisorctl status
securitymonkeyui RUNNING pid 1559, uptime 0:02:55
```

18. Now, let's configure the Celery workers that fetch data from our GCP accounts and look into it for changes:

```
$ sudo cp
/usr/local/src/security_monkey/supervisor/security_monkey_scheduler
.conf /etc/supervisor/conf.d/security_monkey_scheduler.conf
$ sudo systemctl enable supervisor
$ sudo systemctl start supervisor
$ sudo supervisorctl status
securitymonkeyui                    STARTING
securitymonkeyworkers               STARTING
```

If you have trouble starting the workers, verify whether the following command has enough rights to execute:

File: /usr/local/src/security_monkey/supervisor/security_mon
key_scheduler.conf:
command=/usr/local/src/security_monkey/venv/bin/celery -A
security_monkey.task_scheduler.beat.CELERY -s /tmp/sm-
celerybeat-schedule --pidfile=/tmp/sm-celerybeat-
scheduler.pid beat -l debug

19. Finally, the Security Monkey application gets data from our Google Cloud account and the web UI displays the details:

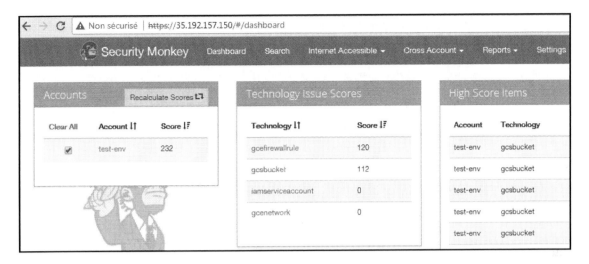

20. In the dashboard of Security Monkey, you can find the security issues identified on our account:

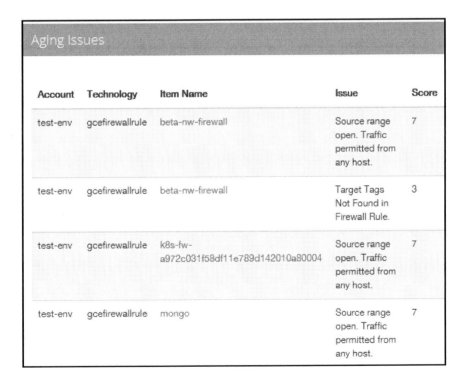

Creating instance backups

Backing up is an important part of any enterprise's business continuity and disaster recovery process. Almost every instance running in an organization is backed up at some frequency that is demanded by the business needs. There are some components of the IT ecosystem that are backed up more often than others. Backing up data lies at a very important level in the spectrum and hence hard disks, data in tables, and configuration data are saved in multiple ways.

In this recipe, we'll simulate a disaster scenario of a Linux instance failing and how we can bring up the machine from its last saved backup. One of the simplest ways to back up a disk on the GCP is by using snapshots. Snapshots take a copy of the disk at a point in time and are efficiently designed to back up data continuously (at requested intervals) via incremental snapshots. Incremental snapshots do not back up the entire disk, but only the data that has changed since the last backup. GCP also offers an easy way to restore the snapshots back into disks that are usable by instances.

Getting ready

The following are the initial setup verification steps before the recipe can be executed:

1. Create or select a GCP project
2. Enable billing and enable the default APIs (some APIs like BigQuery, storage, monitoring, and a few others are enabled automatically)

How to do it...

In this recipe, we'll create a VM with a boot disk and an additional disk. We'll use a script to take a backup of the disks attached to the machine. Then, we'll simulate a total instance failure and try to manually bring back the instance from the backup snapshots:

1. Let's create a Debian Linux instance with an additional disk and make sure that the Compute Engine API has read/write access. The additional disk is created first:

	Name ∧	Type	Size	Zone	In use by	
☐ ⊘	disk-1	Standard persistent disk	10 GB	us-central1-c		⋮

2. The following screenshot shows the created instance:

	Name ∧	Zone	Recommendation	Internal IP	External IP	Connect
☐ ✓	instance-1	us-central1-c		10.128.0.2	104.198.165.213	SSH ▾ ⋮

3. The following screenshot shows the attached disks:

Boot disk and local disks

Name	Size (GB)	Type	Mode
instance-1	10	Standard persistent disk	Boot, read/write

☑ Delete boot disk when instance is deleted

Additional disks

Name	Size (GB)	Type	Mode	When deleting instance
disk-1	10	Standard persistent disk	Read/write	Keep disk

4. The Compute Engine API is in **Read Write** format:

Cloud API access scopes	
BigQuery	Disabled
Bigtable Admin	Disabled
Bigtable Data	Disabled
Cloud Datastore	Disabled
Cloud Debugger	Disabled
Cloud Pub/Sub	Disabled
Cloud Source Repositories	Disabled
Cloud SQL	Disabled
Compute Engine	Read Write
Service Control	Enabled
Service Management	Read Only
Stackdriver Logging API	Write Only
Stackdriver Monitoring API	Write Only
Stackdriver Trace	Write Only
Storage	Read Only
Task queue	Disabled
User info	Disabled

5. We'll use Jack Segal's automatic snapshot script (`https://github.com/` `jacksegal/google-compute-snapshot`) for this purpose. SSH into the GCE instance and execute the following commands to download the script:

```
$ wget
https://raw.githubusercontent.com/jacksegal/google-compute-snapshot
/master/gcloud-snapshot.sh
$ chmod +x gcloud-snapshot.sh
$ sudo mkdir -p /opt/google-compute-snapshot
$ sudo mv gcloud-snapshot.sh /opt/google-compute-snapshot
```

6. Now, let's manually execute the script to take a snapshot of the boot disk (`disk-1`) and the additional disk (`instance-1`):

```
$ sudo /opt/google-compute-snapshot/gcloud-snapshot.sh
2018-04-04 22:25:28: Start of Script
2018-04-04 22:25:28: Start of createSnapshotWrapper
Creating snapshot(s) gcs-disk-1-7023749120190379755-1522880728...
..............done.
Creating snapshot(s) gcs-
instance-1-7023749120190379755-1522880728...
.............................done.
2018-04-04 22:26:12: Start of deleteSnapshotsWrapper
2018-04-04 22:26:14: End of Script
```

7. Create a sample test file on the `home` drive:

```
$ cd ~
$ echo 'Data in file' > data.txt
$ cat data.txt
Data in file
```

8. Let's format the additional disk and add a sample text file in it:

```
$ sudo mkdir /data
$ lsblk
NAME    MAJ:MIN RM SIZE RO TYPE MOUNTPOINT
sda       8:0    0  10G  0 disk
└─sda1    8:1    0  10G  0 part /
sdb       8:16   0  10G  0 disk
$ sudo mkfs.ext4 /dev/sdb
$ sudo mount /dev/sdb /data/
$ sudo chmod a+w /data
$ cd /data
/data$ echo 'sample data in additional disk' > disk1-data.txt
/data$ cat disk1-data.txt
sample data in additional disk
```

9. Run the script again to create a second set of the snapshot for the two disks:

	Name ^	Source disk	Creation time	Disk size	Snapshot size
☐ ⊘	gcs-disk-1-7023749120190379755-1522880728	disk-1		10 GB	0 B
☐ ⊘	gcs-disk-1-7023749120190379755-1522883446	disk-1		10 GB	364.5 KB
☐ ⊘	gcs-instance-1-7023749120190379755-1522880728	instance-1		10 GB	504.86 MB
☐ ⊘	gcs-instance-1-7023749120190379755-1522883446	instance-1		10 GB	8.15 MB

10. Run a Linux command to crash the system in order to simulate an unintended failure:

    ```
    $ sudo rm -rf /boot
    ```

11. Now, if you restart the instance, it will fail to reboot and you won't be able to connect to this instance.

12. To restore the instance to its backed-up state, let's first recreate the additional disk from the snapshot.

13. Create a new disk called `disk-1-bkup` using the snapshot ID:

    ```
    $ gcloud compute snapshots list
    NAME                                                DISK_SIZE_GB
    SRC_DISK                        STATUS
    gcs-disk-1-7023749120190379755-1522880728           10              us-
    central1-c/disks/disk-1         READY
    gcs-disk-1-7023749120190379755-1522883446           10              us-
    central1-c/disks/disk-1         READY
    gcs-instance-1-7023749120190379755-1522880728  10              us-
    central1-c/disks/instance-1   READY
    gcs-instance-1-7023749120190379755-1522883446  10              us-
    central1-c/disks/instance-1   READY
    $ gcloud compute disks create disk-1-bkup --source-snapshot=gcs-
    disk-1-7023749120190379755-1522883446 --zone=us-central1-c
    ```

14. Next, navigate to the latest snapshot of the boot disk (`instance-1`) and click on **CREATE INSTANCE**:

15. Select the same OS, machine type, and API access and attach the newly-created disk (`disk-1-bkup`) to the new instance. The following screenshot shows the creation screen of `instance-2`:

16. Choose the following Compute Engine for API access setup:

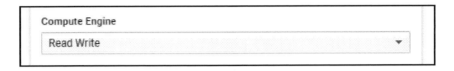

17. Add the following new additional disk:

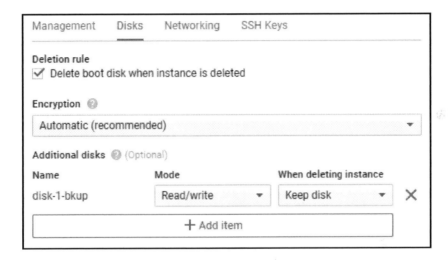

18. SSH into the newly-created instance and verify that the data from the previous snapshot is present:

```
$ ls
data.txt
~$ cat data.txt
Data in file
~$ lsblk
NAME    MAJ:MIN RM SIZE RO TYPE MOUNTPOINT
sda      8:0    0  10G  0 disk
 └─sda1  8:1    0  10G  0 part /
sdb      8:16   0  10G  0 disk
~$ sudo mount /dev/sdb /data/
~$ cd /data/
/data$ ls
disk1-data.txt  lost+found
/data$ cat disk1-data.txt
sample data in additional disk
```

19. Thus, we have simulated a system failure and restored the machine from the snapshots to its old state. The whole process of backing up and restoring from it can be scripted to perform more reliably.

Simulating VM migration

Migrating servers to the cloud is an activity that most enterprises have been engaged with since the dawn of the public cloud. Rehost and refactor are two of the five migration strategies detailed by Gartner that are pertinent for server migration. In this recipe, we'll simulate a rehost of a server. We'll migrate a virtual machine from one project/organization to another manually in order to understand an instance's migration.

Getting ready

The following are the initial setup verification steps before the recipe can be executed:

1. Create or select a GCP project
2. Enable billing and enable the default APIs (some APIs like BigQuery, storage, monitoring, and a few others are enabled automatically)

How to do it...

For this recipe, we'll take a backup of a CentOS VM in RAW virtual disk format. Then, we'll import the virtual disk into our target project and recreate the VM. The following steps explain the creation of the VM:

1. First, let's create a CentOS 7 VM and call this our source instance:

Name ^	Zone	Recommendation	Internal IP	External IP	Connect	
instance-1	us-central1-c		10.128.0.2	35.184.244.82	SSH ▾	⋮

SSH into the instance and print the system information to confirm the Linux version:

```
$ uname -a
Linux instance-1 3.10.0-693.21.1.el7.x86_64 #1 SMP Wed Mar 7
19:03:37 UTC 2018 x86_64 x86_64 x86_64 GNU/Linux
```

2. Create a text file in the home folder and save it:

```
$ echo 'Data in file' > data.txt
$ cat data.txt
Data in file
```

The following steps show the exportation of the source VM's disk to RAW format:

1. Stop the source VM and create a snapshot of the disk attached to the instance:

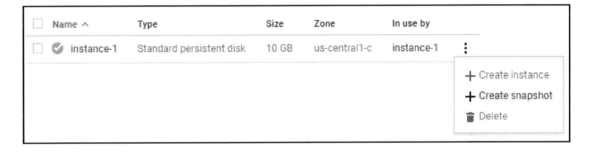

2. Next, create a new disk from the snapshot of the source disk (disk `instance-1`, as seen previously):

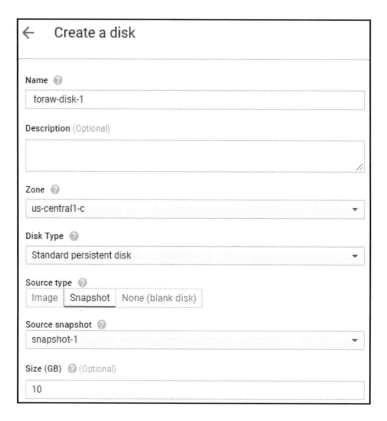

3. Create another temp disk that is 1.5 times the size of the source disk, which is 15 GB in our case. The source disk (`instance-1`), the copied disk (`toraw-disk-1`), and the temporary disk (`temp-disk`) can be seen as follows:

	Name ∧	Type	Size	Zone	In use by	
☐ ✅	instance-1	Standard persistent disk	10 GB	us-central1-c	instance-1	⋮
☐ ✅	temp-disk	Standard persistent disk	15 GB	us-central1-c		⋮
☐ ✅	toraw-disk-1	Standard persistent disk	10 GB	us-central1-c		⋮

4. Create another Linux instance and attach the two new disks we created previously (`temp-disk` and `toraw-disk-1`) to that instance:

5. Do make sure that the instance has Storage **Read/Write** access, which will help us upload the created virtual disk RAW file to Google Storage:

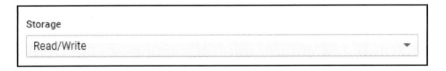

6. Put a new filesystem on the `tmp` disk and mount it:

```
$ lsblk
NAME    MAJ:MIN RM SIZE RO TYPE MOUNTPOINT
sda       8:0    0  10G  0 disk
 └─sda1   8:1    0  10G  0 part /
sdb       8:16   0  10G  0 disk
 └─sdb1   8:17   0  10G  0 part
sdc       8:32   0  15G  0 disk
$ sudo mkfs.ext4 -F /dev/sdc
mke2fs 1.43.4 (31-Jan-2017)
Discarding device blocks: done
```

```
Creating filesystem with 3932160 4k blocks and 983040 inodes
Filesystem UUID: d778d867-8f4f-4151-837a-5aa52a65160c
Superblock backups stored on blocks:
        32768, 98304, 163840, 229376, 294912, 819200, 884736,
1605632, 2654208
Allocating group tables: done
Writing inode tables: done
Creating journal (16384 blocks): done
Writing superblocks and filesystem accounting information: done
$ sudo mkdir /mnt/tmp
$ sudo mount /dev/sdc /mnt/tmp/
```

7. Once the `tmp` disk is prepared, we can create the RAW disk file from the copy of the source disk (`toraw-disk-1`). In the following list of block devices attached to the instance, `sda` is the boot disk and `sdb` will be the copy of our source disk:

```
$ lsblk
NAME     MAJ:MIN RM SIZE RO TYPE MOUNTPOINT
sda       8:0     0  10G  0 disk
 └─sda1   8:1     0  10G  0 part /
sdb       8:16    0  10G  0 disk
 └─sdb1   8:17    0  10G  0 part
sdc       8:32    0  15G  0 disk /mnt/tmp
$ sudo dd if=/dev/sdb of=/mnt/tmp/disk.raw bs=4096
2621440+0 records in
2621440+0 records out
10737418240 bytes (11 GB, 10 GiB) copied, 289.376 s, 37.1 MB/s
lego_gcp@instance-2:~$ cd /mnt/tmp/
lego_gcp@instance-2:/mnt/tmp$ ls
disk.raw  lost+found
```

8. Create an archive of the RAW file and move it to Google Storage:

```
$ cd /mnt/tmp
$ sudo tar czvf myimage.tar.gz disk.raw
disk.raw
$ ls
disk.raw  lost+found  myimage.tar.gz
$ sudo gsutil -o GSUtil:parallel_composite_upload_threshold=150M cp
myimage.tar.gz gs:/
/<Bucket Name>/
Copying file://myimage.tar.gz [Content-Type=application/x-tar]...
\ [1 files][756.3 MiB/756.3 MiB]
Operation completed over 1 objects/756.3 MiB.
```

Follow these steps in order to import the virtual disk to another project:

1. Navigate to another project or another GCP account. Make sure that the current project has access to copy the RAW image file from the Google Storage bucket.
2. In the Google Console, navigate to **Compute Engine** | **Images** and click on **Create image**.
3. In the **Source**, select **Cloud Storage file** and provide the archive of the RAW virtual disk:

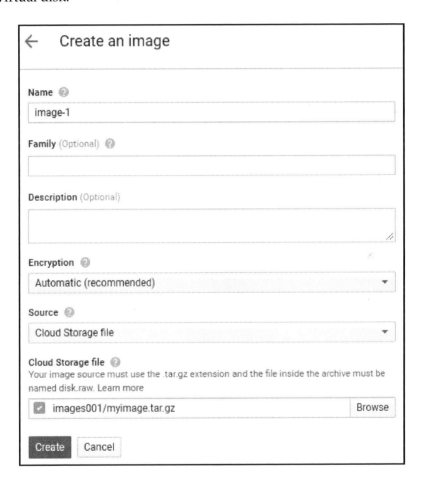

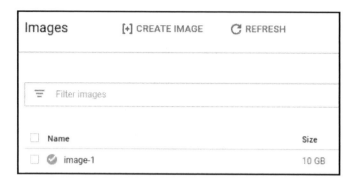

5. Now, you can launch a new instance based on this image:

6. SSH into the newly-restored machine and you'll be able to see the data from the source machine:

```
[@restored-instance ~]$ ls
data.txt
[@restored-instance ~]$ cat data.txt
Data in file
```

Creating a golden image using Packer

Packer is an open source tool that was created by HashiCorp for creating images. It works on most of the cloud platforms and is well integrated with the most popular configuration management tools. Packer understands the target environment and creates images to fit well on the target cloud platform. Creating images for standard use for development and also for applications is a common task at the enterprise level. While burning images for standard VMs, security and enterprise policies can be baked into the image. For application images, new images can be created for every release/version of the software. This helps in traceability and building robust systems.

Getting ready

The following are the initial setup verification steps before the recipe can be executed:

1. Create or select a GCP project
2. Enable billing and enable the default APIs (some APIs like BigQuery, storage, monitoring, and a few others are enabled automatically)

How to do it...

In this recipe, we'll create a temporary machine and install Packer. Then, we'll create the necessary configuration files for Packer to create an image running PHP:

1. To run Packer, let's first create a Debian GNU/Linux 9 instance with **Read/Write** access to **Compute Engine** and **Full** access to **Storage**:

2. SSH into the newly-created machine and install Packer (the binaries are available in packer.io):

```
$ cd ~
$ sudo apt-get install unzip
$ wget
https://releases.hashicorp.com/packer/1.2.2/packer_1.2.2_linux_amd6
4.zip
$ unzip packer_1.2.2_linux_amd64.zip
$ ls
packer packer_1.2.2_linux_amd64.zip
```

```
$ ./packer
Usage: packer [--version] [--help] <command> [<args>]
Available commands are:
    build         build image(s) from template
    fix           fixes templates from old versions of packer
    inspect       see components of a template
    push          push a template and supporting files to a Packer
build service
    validate      check that a template is valid
    version       Prints the Packer version
```

3. Once Packer is successfully installed, we can create our configuration file. The first part of the configuration is the builder. The builder defines the instance that will be created and then turned into an image. For this example, we have chosen a Debian 9 Linux machine and hence all the commands are related to this version of the operating system. For authentication, Packer uses the service account of the base instance in order to create the image. Alternatively, we can also provide a credential file for authentication. The following is the golden.json file:

```json
{
  "builders": [
    {
      "type": "googlecompute",
      "project_id": "bold-future-200221",
      "source_image": "debian-9-stretch-v20180401",
      "ssh_username": "debian",
      "zone": "us-central1-a"
    }
  ],
    "provisioners": [
        {
            "type": "shell",
            "inline":[
                "sudo apt-get install -y apache2",
                "sudo apt-get install -y php git",
                "sudo systemctl restart apache2"
            ]
        },
        {
            "type": "shell",
            "script": "./pull-code.sh"
        }
    ]
}
```

4. The `provisioner` section of the configuration uses shell commands/shell scripts to perform our desired operation. In the inline shell commands we used previously, we installed the prerequisites for a web server to run PHP.

5. The second part of the `provisioner` section is a shell script that simulates a code pull and places the code in the appropriate folder. The following is the `pull-code.sh` file:

```
#!/bin/bash
echo "<?php phpinfo(); ?>" | sudo tee --append
/var/www/html/info.php
#cd /var/www/html
#sudo git clone https://github.com/banago/simple-php-website.git
sudo systemctl restart apache2
```

6. With the two files (`golden.json` and `pull-code.sh`) present, we can now run Packer to create the image:

```
$ ./packer validate golden.json
Template validated successfully.
$ ./packer build golden.json
googlecompute output will be in this color.
==> googlecompute: Checking image does not exist...
==> googlecompute: Creating temporary SSH key for instance...
==> googlecompute: Using image: debian-9-stretch-v20180401
==> googlecompute: Creating instance...
    googlecompute: Loading zone: us-central1-a
    googlecompute: Loading machine type: n1-standard-1
    googlecompute: Requesting instance creation...
    googlecompute: Waiting for creation operation to complete...
    googlecompute: Instance has been created!
==> googlecompute: Waiting for the instance to become running...
    googlecompute: IP: 35.192.211.243
...
==> googlecompute: Provisioning with shell script: ./pull-code.sh
    googlecompute: <?php phpinfo(); ?>
==> googlecompute: Deleting instance...
    googlecompute: Instance has been deleted!
==> googlecompute: Creating image...
==> googlecompute: Deleting disk...
    googlecompute: Disk has been deleted!
Build 'googlecompute' finished.
==> Builds finished. The artifacts of 1successful builds are:
--> googlecompute: A disk image was created: packer-1523057779
```

7. You can view the created image in the GCP Console:

Name	Size
✅ packer-1523057779	10 GB

8. Finally, to verify our golden image, you can create an instance (allow HTTP access) based on the image created and verify the functionality:

← Images   🗑 DELETE   ➕ CREATE INSTANCE

packer-1523057779

Description
Created by Packer

Creation time
7 Apr 2018, 01:39:28

Encryption
Automatic

Equivalent REST

9. Using the IP of the of the newly-created machine, if you point the browser to the URL `http://<IP>/info.php`, it should open the `info.php` page:

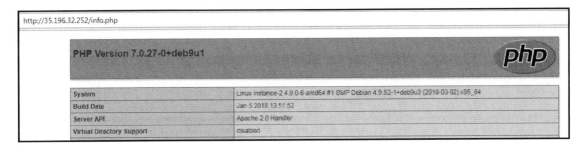

http://35.196.32.252/info.php

PHP Version 7.0.27-0+deb9u1

System	Linux instance-2 4.9 0-6-amd64 #1 SMP Debian 4.9.82-1+deb9u3 (2018-03-02) x86_64
Build Date	Jan 5 2018 13:51:52
Server API	Apache 2.0 Handler
Virtual Directory Support	disabled

Other Books You May Enjoy

If you enjoyed this book, you may be interested in these other books by Packt:

Google Cloud Platform for Developers
Ted Hunter

ISBN: 978-1-78883-767-5

- Gain a deep understanding of the various service offerings on GCP and when to use them.
- Deploy and run services on managed platforms such as App Engine and Container Engine.
- Securely maintain application state with Cloud SQL, Cloud Storage, Datastore, and Bigtable.
- Leverage StackDriver monitoring and debugging to minimize downtime and mitigate issues without impacting users.
- Design and implement complex software solutions utilizing the full power of Google Cloud.
- Integrate with best-in-class Big Data solutions such as Bigquery, Dataflow, and Pub/Sub.

Google Cloud Platform for Architects
Vitthal Srinivasan, Janani Ravi, Judy Raj

ISBN: 978-1-78883-430-8

- Set up GCP account and get detailed knowledge of Cloud Shell and its usage.
- Create and edit VM instance along with Kubernetes cluster followed by Continuous deployment with Jenkins.
- Overcome the object impedance mismatch with NoSQL databases.
- Migrate programs to machines on the cloud without fundamentally restructuring code or processes.
- Get insights about the health, performance, and availability of cloud-powered applications with the help of monitoring, logging and diagnostic tools in Stackdriver.

Leave a review - let other readers know what you think

Please share your thoughts on this book with others by leaving a review on the site that you bought it from. If you purchased the book from Amazon, please leave us an honest review on this book's Amazon page. This is vital so that other potential readers can see and use your unbiased opinion to make purchasing decisions, we can understand what our customers think about our products, and our authors can see your feedback on the title that they have worked with Packt to create. It will only take a few minutes of your time, but is valuable to other potential customers, our authors, and Packt. Thank you!

Index